'The tongue-in-cheek phrase *Top T...* honestly and candidly, one individual's journey from sexual shame and gender dysphoria, to gender and sexual autonomy. This uncompromising tale inspires and challenges us. As a trans man myself, Finn has always encouraged and motivated me. For helping to dispel fear and those accompanying ghost stories, thank you can never convey enough! A must read for anyone considering lower surgery and those who support us.'

– *Dr Wenn B. Lawson (PhD) CPsychol AFBPsS MAPs*

'*Top To Bottom* is a wonderful trans memoir and a greatly needed resource for anyone considering phalloplasty. Much more than that though, Finlay's book is a human story of the move towards authenticity and belonging. Told with great warmth, humour and self-awareness, it's a cracking read for anybody.'

– Meg-John Barker, *author of* How to Understand Your Gender *and* Gender: A Graphic Guide

'*Top To Bottom* - a story you've never heard before but a story that needs to be told. This memoir is universally written, acting as an outstanding guide to any trans man about to embark on this journey, but also as a fascinating insight into the complexity of being human. Finn is an extraordinary writer, his tone is warm, painfully honest, profound and humorous. I'll be highly recommending this book for years to come.'

– *Ash Palmisciano, TV actor and speaker*

'Finn has given us a gift. A timely companion on the journey to advocate for one's own pleasure, hone the hoop-jumping skills needed to medically affirm one's gender and to nurture the community needed to raise a penis!'

– *Dr Liam 'Captain' Snowdon, genderqueerdo & co-founder of the Institute for the Study of Somatic Sex Education*

Top To Bottom

A Memoir and Personal Guide
Through Phalloplasty

Finlay Games

Jessica Kingsley Publishers
London and Philadelphia

First published in Great Britain in 2021 by Jessica Kingsley Publishers
An Hachette Company

1

The information contained in this book is not intended to replace
the services of trained medical professionals or to be a substitute for
medical advice. You are advised to consult a doctor on any matters
relating to your health, and in particular on any matters that may
require diagnosis or medical attention.

Trigger warning: This book describes in-depth surgical procedures.

A CIP catalogue record for this title is available from the British
Library and the Library of Congress

ISBN 978 1 78775 587 1
eISBN 978 1 78775 588 8

Printed and bound in the United States
by West Publishing Corporation

Jessica Kingsley Publishers' policy is to use papers that are natural,
renewable and recyclable products and made from wood grown
in sustainable forests. The logging and manufacturing processes
are expected to conform to the environmental regulations of
the country of origin.

Jessica Kingsley Publishers
Carmelite House
50 Victoria Embankment
London EC4Y 0DZ

www.jkp.com

This memoir is dedicated to all the transgender people
who generously shared their experiences of lower surgery.
Your stories were a light in an otherwise dark tunnel, and I
can never thank you enough. It is with your courage in mind
that I now pay this debt forward.

The names of everyone save for the author have been changed.

Contents

Acknowledgements

Writing a memoir is no easy task, especially when that memoir is about your penis. I want to thank everyone, especially the 'FinnFam' who reminded me that this book was needed. You helped me to overcome my fears and just get it written.

A huge thank you, especially, to the team at St Peter's Andrology Centre. Managing the ever-growing population of trans people opting for surgery is no easy task. And to all the surgeons, thank you for bringing Finn Jr. to life. I hope this book will demonstrate the enormous impact your skilled workmanship has on improving trans people's lives.

To my publishers, thank you for agreeing to give this book a home. I have every faith that it will be safe in your hands and reach the people who need it most.

To my mum, thank you for passing on your 'Duracell® Bunny' genes. I am incredibly grateful to have inherited your resilient body, and I am thankful that you stayed alive long enough to see me happy inside it. I know if you were alive, you would think this book was 'bloody brilliant'.

To my dear friends, Ben, Clair, Kris, Michelle and Patrick, I

am forever grateful to you all for taking our friendship to the next level, by kindly agreeing to read through early drafts of this book. I am especially grateful to those of you who shared time with me during my 'sexual summer'. I was often unmanageably excited, and you were always supportive and patient.

To my 'it's a man's world' brothers, haven't we all come such a long way! Sharing a late second puberty with you all made going through this rollercoaster journey just that little bit less terrifying. I am proud to call you my brothers and I love you all very much.

To my generous 'husband and wife', Ryan and Lucy, thank you for making your spare room mine and taking such good care of me. Who knew cheese sandwiches and soup could taste so good together? Thank you also to your mum for the amazing cakes. My thanks also to the four fur children for standing guard and purring away my post-op blues.

Thank you to Alex. I wish we hadn't ended as we did, but I will be forever grateful to you for taking care of me through the enormity of stage one recovery. I am especially grateful to you for instigating the questions surrounding my sexuality. As you always told me, what is for you doesn't go past you.

To Erin, there will never be enough words to express how thankful I am to you for waking me up in every way possible. My lower surgery journey might not have been as magical and transformative, had our paths not crossed.

To Owen and Frankie, thank you for trusting me enough to let me share your relationship for a brief time, and for bravely sharing your bodies with me.

And finally, but most importantly, to my giggle buddy, best friend, and soulmate, Jamie. It has been through your eyes that my internal image and knowledge of myself as a man is forever cemented into my soul. It is also through you that I have come

to know the beauty of what true love and a healthy relationship is. Thank you for your unwavering belief in me and for standing by me in everything I do, even when I decide to stick my penis on bookshelves.

Preface

This entire book is about my penis. This is my story of going through lower surgery, specifically phalloplasty, and the adventures I have had with my changing genitals along the way. You may be wondering why my penis needs an entire book. Why didn't I just write my transgender memoir in its entirety, from start to finish, and include my lower surgery process in that? It is a valid question.

When I started my phalloplasty journey, I decided that I would document my experiences. There was little first-hand information available and I wanted to bridge that gap. As I began to share my honest experiences on my YouTube channel and blog, it became clear that people were crying out for the information. I decided then, to take things a step further and turn my documentation into a book. My aim was to write the kind of book I wished I'd had access to when I started my journey.

I wanted to address the lack of information about lower surgery, and address some of the myths that still exist. I avoided even thinking about lower surgery for years because of the horror stories I had heard. There was no end of tales of surgical

complications and penises with a Frankenstein appearance. Then, when I discovered that successful surgery and an aesthetically pleasing penis was possible, the lack of information was a huge barrier to making informed choices.

When I began my lower surgery journey, few people were sharing openly about their experiences. I could find some statistics and medical information, but what I lacked were honest experiences from trans people who had gone through the surgery process. As I tentatively began my journey, the lack of information made it difficult to make decisions. The lack of information also made it difficult to know what to look out for during the healing process. Therefore, I decided I wanted to share my journey in detail, so that I might be a source of reference, support and guidance for others on their lower surgery journey.

The second reason my penis needed an entire book was because the process of lower surgery is far more than just a physical one. For me, phalloplasty didn't just involve a process of surgery and physical recovery; it was also a process of emotional growth and healing. Whilst my entire transition has changed my life, it was the arrival of my penis which really changed everything.

With the arrival of my penis, I began to heal from a lifetime of sexual confusion. I began to feel embodied for the first time. I began to enjoy my body in the hands of others. My penis also helped me to realize and come to terms with the fact that my main sexual attraction is towards men. Being embodied and finding my sexual self has played a huge part in overcoming my dysphoria. The lowering of dysphoria has in turn helped me to better manage the mental health issues that I have lived with all my life. In a body that outwardly reflects the truth of who I am, I have felt at home for the first time. This internal safe space has made it possible to do the healing that I could not access

before I had lower surgery. Therefore to do this journey justice, the experience needed to be captured in its own book, separate from the rest of my transition.

However, it is important to note that the fact that I have dedicated an entire book to my penis does not mean that lower surgery is the most important part of the transgender journey. Phalloplasty was a significant part of my journey to wholeness and to overcome dysphoria, but that may not be everyone's experience. Not all trans people want lower surgery, and not wanting surgery does not make you any less trans nor any less male.

This book is designed to be both a memoir and guide. It is intended primarily for trans people exploring and going through lower surgery. However, it may also be of help to the loved ones of trans people, and others seeking to better understand trans lives. As a memoir, my aim is for this book to give an insight into how profoundly surgery can change a life; that, far from being cosmetic, the surgeries some trans people go through are both life-saving and life-enhancing. The aim of this book is to act as a guide to help people exploring lower surgery options and serve as a companion through the journey. I hope that it might help to dispel some of the many myths which exist about lower surgery. I also hope it may show that phalloplasty doesn't result in a numb, Frankenstein penis monster.

Finding statistics to be of little help, I have mostly steered away from them. As a psychology student, quantitative data, which measures only in numbers, always felt lacking to me. I felt this lack keenly when trying to use quantitative data to explore lower surgery. Statistics are just brief snapshots in time. Numbers are forever changing and tell us nothing about experience. On the other hand, qualitative data, which is concerned with lived experience, is rich and tangible. The most valuable sources of information in my journey were the first-hand accounts of

people going through surgery. Knowing how people made decisions, how they later felt about those decisions, how they coped through surgery – these were the things which helped me. It is for these reasons that this book concentrates fully on the lived experience of the lower surgery journey and steers away from statistics and medical jargon.

Do please note that I am not a trained medical professional, so if you are ever unsure about anything, please do check things out with your doctor or consultant. This book is not designed to be a replacement for medical care. You must always follow your consultant's advice.

Ultimately, this book aims to give a very honest and balanced account of the entire physical and emotional processes involved in the lower surgery journey. Told from my own experience and point of view, this is an account of real events. However, the way I remember events may differ from those who shared them with me. I have done my best to recreate my journey from memory, and from my journals and videos, and I have used creativity when my memory failed me. I have changed the names of everyone mentioned in the book to protect their anonymity. I have also changed some of the locations and other identifying characteristics.

Before we get stuck in, a note on language. I have tried throughout this book to make the language as inclusive as possible. However, language changes all the time and there may be terms written here that later become problematic. Please know that I have done my best, at the time, to use language that aims to be as inclusive as possible.

I have used the word 'trans' or 'transgender' to describe myself and others. I do often switch between using 'trans men/man' and 'trans people'. This is because I want to acknowledge that not all people who go through lower surgery procedures identify

as male. Non-binary people, for example, can, and do, choose to have lower surgery.

There are also many occasions when I have used various words to describe my genitals. Through my journey, in dealing with dysphoria, I have used words which felt comfortable at the time and reflected where I was in my personal growth. These words are just my personal preferences and it should be noted that these will not be the same for every trans person. My hope is that if the language is not to your taste, you will be able to overlook it to see the message underneath.

And finally, please remember that this is just one person's experience. Whilst I hope that you will find commonality here, my story is just one narrative among a huge kaleidoscope of trans experiences. Although many of our destinations are the same, our journeys are not.

I wish you all the luck in the world with yours.

Finn

Awakening to the Absence of My Penis

I was adamant that I would not be having any kind of lower surgery as part of my gender transition. 'The penis does not maketh the man,' I would proudly state when asked if I was having *The Surgery*. You know, *The Surgery*: the one where we wave with a grin of reckless abandon like a contestant on *Stars in Their Eyes*; we exit stage left, then return through smoke-filled double doors, a gleaming personification of all a man can be, accompanied by a chorus of 'oohs' and 'ahs'.

It's a rather large myth (no pun intended) that all trans people have The Surgery. For a start, The Surgery doesn't actually exist. There are a lot of different types of surgery and some trans people choose not to have surgery at all. Having surgery is not a requirement of being transgender; each trans person differs on the path they follow, depending on how they feel about their identity and how they present.

When I realized I was transgender, in 2011 at the relatively late age of 37, the last thing I was concerned about was my penis, or lack thereof. When I began the process of coming out, my full focus was on gaining approval for hormones. My external

appearance was my main concern, and only cross-sex hormones could change that.

I had briefly looked at lower surgery options but more out of curiosity than for anything else. There wasn't much information available about lower surgery at the time and it seemed that very few trans men opted to have it. The scant information I found suggested that lower surgery was a long, complicated and painful journey. There were only a few cases I could find of trans men who'd had it and were happy. However, the over-riding consensus was that lower surgery was highly risky and often unsuccessful. It wasn't uncommon to find lower surgery described as creating little more than a Frankenstein monster. I felt lucky that it wasn't something I would ever need.

I was often told – by the few men I could find who had chosen to have lower surgery – that my thoughts about it would change further down the line, especially after having top surgery. (Top surgery, or chest reconstruction, is the term most trans people prefer, to describe when a surgeon performs a double mastectomy to create a male-defined chest.) However, I was adamant about not needing lower surgery – so much so that I doubted very much if a post-surgery penis desire would happen to me. I assured people that I was different, that I did not feel the need for a penis and would not be going there.

It's important to point out that needing and wanting are two entirely separate things. My need was not there, because at the time I was not aware of any lower dysphoria. However, that's not to say I didn't want a penis. If it were as simple as growing my own, had there been a magical way to alter my genes so that a penis appeared, I would have jumped at the chance. However, I simply could not face the lengthy surgery, and all the risks and sacrifices involved.

Besides this, I was also in a relationship at the time with

someone who identified as a lesbian. Jen and I had met as two women and started dating a year before I came out as transgender. Although my coming out had initially been a shock, Jen had been incredibly understanding of my transition. However, neither of us knew if our relationship would survive, as I changed from the woman she had first met into the man I knew myself to be. I think, in some ways, my insistence that I wouldn't be having any kind of lower surgery was to reassure her and to avoid the prospect of losing her. We later split up anyway, which was less to do with transition and more to do with growing apart, but I'll come to that later.

Still, I did prepare myself after my top surgery, just in case the need for a penis arrived. However, all I felt after top surgery was utter joy at finally having my true chest revealed. The feeling of seeing myself bare-chested, to no longer need to turn away in disgust from my own flesh, was exhilarating. My feelings towards my genitals did change, but in terms of acceptance of the parts I had, rather than an increase in dysphoria. The increase in my sense of masculinity was so powerful that my otherwise differently configured body was not an issue.

By the time I had top surgery, it was 2012. I had been on testosterone for seven months and my features had changed significantly. Being consistently correctly gendered, combined with my new chest, gave me more confidence in my male identity. I had also grown quite a substantial T-dick, where the testosterone causes the clitoris to enlarge and resemble a mini-penis. All these changes coming together meant I found I could view my genitals neutrally and see them as male parts despite not looking like a penis. These parts are on me, I am male, therefore they are my male parts.

However, this new joy in my body was short-lived. As I progressed through my transition and settled more into an

embodied state of knowing myself to be a man, rather than just thinking I felt like one, I began to feel the absence of my penis.

To outsiders not knowing the life of a trans person, it may seem confusing how a person can live as one gender and not know that they need to go through transition or to have surgery, until much later in life. How can one be missing a male body and not know it?

This is something I had to ask myself in my early days of discovering myself to be trans and in the lead-up to every surgery. How could I have lived until 37 years of age and not know I was male? I've come to make sense of this by using an analogy of a prison cell. If all you have ever known is the inside of a small cell, this is your home. Although you may have a sense that there is something more, a sense of ill-ease inside yourself perhaps, you cannot know why because you cannot imagine what might be missing. Then, once someone shows you what is outside that cell, suddenly everything makes sense and now you desperately want that freedom for yourself. That cell can never again feel like home, and your perspective is forever changed.

Discovering I was transgender was my first peek outside that prison cell. Suddenly, I could make sense of the years of anguish. I was male, but the outward female appearance of my body was holding my male self prisoner. Announcing myself as male was my stepping outside the cell. However, to then be truly free I had to find my own way forward. What did I need in this new life to be the man I had always been inside? And this is where our different trans journeys come into play. We all need different things, to bring our outward presentation in line with our gender identity. And we all need to discover what we need to transform our body from a prison cell to a home. There is no set way to know this; our needs manifest as we take our first mindful steps on our journey to freedom.

The first manifestation of my awareness of my lack of penis was in using a packer (a type of prosthetic penis). At the time I started using a packer, which was just a couple of months after I came out as trans, I didn't connect the experience I had to a lack of penis as such. Rather, I thought it was about helping me to feel more confident in my male gender identity.

Like every trans person I know, in my early days I was obsessed with 'passing'. (I no longer use this term – it is one I do not like. The trouble with the term 'passing' is that it implies we are dressing up as something we are not. I was never trying to pass as a man; I was trying to get people to see I was already a man. That's why I now prefer the term 'being read correctly'.) So, in the early days of my transition, before the hormones had turned my soft baby face into the hairy one it is today, I wanted something to help signal my maleness to others.

Living with gender dysphoria (the term for the feeling of the mismatch between your assigned gender at birth and the gender you identify as) is utter hell. Every 'Can I help you, miss?' is like a punch to the gut. So, to help to give myself a sense of confidence in my maleness and to try to get people to gender me correctly, I decided to try out a packer. Packers can range from the most basic novelty style, only slightly resembling the real thing, through to highly detailed realistic penises, designed specifically for trans guys. These can function as just a soft packer, to give a bulge in your pants, or to be much more functional as a stand-to-pee device. Some of them can even function for sexual intercourse.

As my packer was to be used as little more than a sophisticated bulge, I went with the most basic kind, the unfortunately named 'Mr. Limpy™'. I also hoped that this bulge in my trousers would help me walk in a more masculine way. What a masculine walk is I don't know, but at the time I thought I needed one.

The decision to buy a packer was all based around my need to be seen as male and to use it to give me confidence, rather than it being about replacing a part I felt was missing.

However, further down the line, this began to change, and the sense that I was missing something began to dawn on me. It started with the arrival of my sex drive, at around seven weeks on testosterone. To say my sex drive 'arrived' is a bit of an understatement – rather, it crashed through the front door like an embarrassingly drunk uncle at a family get-together.

Up until that point, I had never had much of a sex drive. Sex was a common cause of arguments in all my relationships, including my relationship with Jen at the time. I could do without sex, to be honest, and if I masturbated twice a year that would do me nicely, thanks. Suddenly, seven times a day wasn't enough.

I woke one morning on what initially seemed like an 'ordinary' day. I mean ordinary aside from the fact that I had been on testosterone for seven weeks. Every day at that stage was rather exciting as it involved daily hunts for new hair growth and a thorough examination of my face in the mirror. I was, however, surprised to realize I had woken up with a stiffy. Yes, an actual stiffy. By this point, my T-dick had begun to grow significantly. It was swollen and protruding and at times a little sensitive. That morning, it was rock hard. It may have been no bigger than the top of my thumb, but it was as hard as a bullet. It took me a while to work out that the warm sensation that had entirely gripped the lower half of my body was sexual arousal. It's safe to say I got very little done for the rest of that day and in the weeks that followed.

On one particular unmanageably sexually aroused day during those weeks, instead of reaching in my boxers for my T-dick, I instinctively grabbed my packer and began to wank with it.

I came almost instantly, which was a surprise, but the biggest surprise was that I felt as though I had ejaculated. Rather than being felt internally as my usual orgasms were, I had the sensation of something pulsing through my clenched fist as I wanked and came. The sensation was so real, that when I found my hand to be dry, I even looked around me, to see if something had shot out and landed somewhere. It hadn't.

As I sat there, mouth agape, I grabbed my packer again. At that moment, that packer was not Mr. Limpy™, the novelty silicone toy. It was my penis. It felt connected to me. The shape my hand took around my packer felt like that was the shape my body should be taking. It was such a deeply embodied feeling of correctness in how my body was moving and being held. It felt in every way like a phantom penis, something I had heard other trans guys mention but which I had never personally experienced until then. From that moment my relationship with my lower half began to change. I wanted that experience again because it had felt so right. Suddenly, using my old parts in any way felt so incredibly wrong.

This new realization made me wonder if my inability to enjoy intimacy was more about the lack of a penis rather than a lack of interest in sex than I had previously thought. Before this moment, I hadn't used a strap-on for sex with partners. After a couple of brief attempts in the past (pre-transition), I had dismissed strap-ons as useless. As a proud anti-penis lesbian, I would declare I didn't need a phallic object to satisfy my partner. I now wonder if this had been an unconscious denial of my being transgender.

The combination of these experiences – the sudden fascination with making myself cum by playing with my packer, and the huge dysphoria around my inability to use the urinals – made me look again at the various prosthetics available. Having

previously ruled out dildos and strap-ons, the discovery of this new way of being connected to an invisible phantom penis made me think that a more realistic-looking prosthetic could be the way forward. Perhaps it would also improve mine and Jen's sex life.

I looked at the range of realistic prosthetics – ones that you could glue on and which would stay put for days. I especially liked the three-in-one, multi-functional devices that could go from being soft to erect for penetrative sex and for urinating through, thereby enabling you to pee standing up. However, those were far too expensive and so I finally settled on the Peecock Gen2™ pack-pee-and-play device. It had to be worn with a harness, but the harness was more similar to a pair of pants, and so nothing like the strap-on I had briefly used in the past. The Peecock™ came with a silicone rod which you inserted to make it erect for sex and which had a special 'pleasure area' designed to rub against the clitoris during sex. After my recent experiences with the simple Mr. Limpy™, I felt confident that getting pleasure would not be an issue.

The two weeks waiting for my Peecock™ to arrive felt like forever. On returning home one day to find the discreet brown parcel, I couldn't tear it open quickly enough. The Peecock™ wasn't as realistic as some other prosthetics – more recent versions I've seen are so much better – but it was realistic enough for me. I put it on, using the jock harness I had bought, and stood in front of the mirror. I loved how it looked, hanging loosely between my legs. I wiggled my hips, so that it swung left to right and slapped against my thighs. I grinned like a Cheshire cat.

First things first, I needed to learn to pee with it. I had been advised to try in the shower first, as getting used to the right pee flow rate without causing backflow could apparently be a tough skill to master. I prepared myself by guzzling a pint of water.

I managed to pee in the shower, with no issue whatsoever. I then downed a couple more pints of water so I could have another attempt, this time in the toilet. Finally, having enough of an urge to pee to justify going, I stood, prosthetic penis in hand, facing the toilet, took a deep breath and let go. I managed successfully not to piss myself and felt rather pleased to have mastered it so quickly. I couldn't wait to try it out in public.

Jen and I were off out that night to a gig, so I excitedly dressed, finding a comfortable way to hang my penis. Was I a hang-to-the-left or hang-to-the-right man? The rigidity of the Peecock™, compared with the Mr. Limpy™, made it a challenge to find a comfortable position. With it hanging to one side, you could still make out the line of the prosthetic. That wouldn't do. Instead, I positioned it more downward and slightly to the left. I loved the way it felt and the way the much bigger bulge looked.

The gig venue had unisex toilets. I was quite pleased about this as I was still having issues about being read correctly. I was still so early on in my transition, after all. However, I was a little disappointed not to be able to try a urinal. Still, I did at least get to try in public. It was far more nerve-racking, I can tell you. Once I started peeing, I was glad that it was in a private, locked cubical as it was vastly different from peeing at home. If I pissed myself at home, I could change. If I pissed myself here, I would be in a rather embarrassing situation. What if I had an accident? I had purposely brought a jumper, thinking that if I did have back-flow issues I could tie the jumper around my waist to hide it. I managed to go but I couldn't empty my bladder completely, so it wasn't long before I had to go again. It took a few attempts to be able to let go properly and empty my bladder every time. It took a much longer time to feel confident enough to use it at a urinal, but once I did, it made a huge difference

to my dysphoria, and my ability to socialize without worrying about toilet situations.

Wanking with the Peecock™ was also amazing, but it didn't prove to be great for sex. I had bought the smallest of options, as I didn't want to look like I had an elephant's trunk in my trousers; but, at just 4 inches, it was a little short for sex. Still, Jen and I made it work, and when we did it was good. But the real issue was more our sexual problems than the size of the Peecock™. I'd had a lot of issues with sex throughout my entire life, which at the beginning of my transition I never fully understood. Initially, I thought they were to do with dysphoria. Whilst a large part of my sexual discomfort was likely to do with my discomfort with my body, I would later discover that a larger part was to do with confusion about my sexual attraction. We will come to that later.

I also think now, on reflection, that I couldn't connect to my packer through my partner in the way that I could when I was holding it in my hand and wanking, I think I needed the visual and tactile connection, which made me feel like it was my penis and connected to me, in a way that sex with it could never give. I can clearly see now that this was an early sign that I was missing a penis. At the time, though, its significance to me, as far as I told myself, was about making me more confident and comfortable, rather than fulfilling a need for something I perceived as missing. The Peecock™ solved many issues for me, in boosting my confidence and allowing me to access male toilets with far less dysphoria. Therefore, I pushed any concerns about my lack of a penis to one side.

However, in the months that followed my recovery from top surgery, as stomach-churning, breath-stealing chest dysphoria became increasingly more absent, in its place awakened lower dysphoria and an increased sense of incongruence between my top half and my lower half. By the summer of 2013, my mood had

dropped as my dysphoria spiked. Suddenly, holding my packer in my hand became a source of distress rather than comfort, peeing through it became annoying rather than liberating, and taking it off at night and seeing my lifeless dick on the side of the sink felt humiliating and degrading. For the first time, I looked at my packer and it represented a part of me that was lost.

This really took me by surprise, and it was a while before I could make sense of it. I mean, how could I suddenly feel this amount of dysphoria? Was it my imagination? Surely if it had always been there, I would have felt it before?

I have now made sense of this sudden increase in dysphoria and I believe it was a combination of things. Firstly, I had such severe chest dysphoria that the amount of noise it caused in my mind, and the way it made me disassociate from my body, meant that any lower dysphoria was drowned out by it. Secondly, the shift from feeling like I was a man to knowing I am a man increased even more after top surgery. I never experienced my top surgery as losing something, or having something removed; instead, I viewed my surgery as having something revealed. My true male chest had been there all along, hiding underneath. Finally, being able to see my true chest increased my confidence and my knowledge of myself as a man. This, in turn, made me realize that it wasn't so much that I wanted a penis, but rather that I was missing my penis and I needed to do whatever it took to fix that.

Finding the Right Penis

Exploring Lower Surgery Options

Realizing that I needed lower surgery was a difficult reality to accept. The implications were massive – for my life, my health, and my relationship with Jen. And realizing that I needed surgery was only the start. Knowing I wanted and needed a penis was one thing; but choosing which surgery to have was quite another.

There are two main types of lower surgery: metoidioplasty (meta) and phalloplasty (phallo). In a very brief nutshell (oh the puns), metoidioplasty uses the growth of the clitoris on testosterone to create a micro-penis. Phalloplasty, resulting in an average-size penis, is created from skin taken from a graft on your body. Within these two types, there are also various options, such as where the skin graft is taken from, choosing whether to have a hysterectomy (removal of the uterus and cervix), oophorectomy (removal of the fallopian tubes and ovaries), vaginectomy (removal of the skin lining of the vagina and closure of the vaginal opening), scrotoplasty (creation of testicles using the labia majora), urethral lengthening and burial of the T-dick.

With all these decisions, it's easy to see why working out which surgery I wanted left me rocking in a corner. It was all incredibly overwhelming and terrifying. Unlike top surgery, which is straightforward in comparison, in lower surgery there is so much more to consider. This is one of the main reasons why so many trans men choose not to opt for it. I've spoken to so many guys who say the same thing: it isn't that they don't want a penis; it's rather that they don't want the long surgical process or the associated risks (of which there are many).

Whichever surgery I chose would take years to complete. The idea of having constant surgery for the foreseeable future was not a pleasant one. I was just starting to get my life in order. I had been unemployed for many years due to severe mental health issues and addiction. Going through transition had greatly improved my mental health. I had been sober and clean since 2010, a year before I came out as trans. Finally, in a better place mentally, I was making steps towards getting back to work. I had returned to study – to retrain and work towards a degree in Psychology – and I planned to find some volunteer work to gain experience. I was lucky in some ways – I was a distance-learning student with The Open University, so at least I could be flexible. However, surgery would still have a huge impact on my studies and would make returning to work very difficult. Who would employ me with surgery deadlines looming?

Then there was the risk to my health to consider and the fact that lower surgery had such a poor reputation. All I had ever heard or read were horror stories. Even some of my closest friends had warned me about it. It seemed everyone knew someone who had been disfigured for life or regretted having surgery in the first place. Discussions on trans forums threw the term 'Frankenstein' around a lot, when talking about phalloplasty. Furthermore, I was getting on a bit. Okay, 40 isn't old, but asking

my body, which had been through a lot during those 40 years, to go through the massive upheaval of surgery was a big ask.

My relationship with Jen was further muddling my thoughts and causing a great deal of worry. Jen and I had so far managed to negotiate my transition and my changes. However, it had brought up a great deal for Jen in terms of her own identity. It had taken her many years to come out as a lesbian. My transition and living as male had effectively changed Jen's identity from a lesbian to a straight woman again. We had muddled through and managed to arrive at a comfortable place where my being a man was something Jen accepted. However, I wasn't sure that a penis would be very much welcomed. A penis would change the whole dynamic between us in terms of intimacy and I wasn't sure our relationship could survive that. In discussing my relationship concerns with a friend, I was asked, 'What happens if you have the surgery and you and Jen split up – do you not worry about being able to find another partner?'

I am not going to lie. Of course, that idea terrified me. I loved Jen; she was my best friend as well as my partner. We had known each other for years – even before we started going out – and I didn't want us to split up. Her acceptance of me was incredible and I worried that, as a trans person, I might face a lifetime alone if we split up. What if nobody else could accept my past or my differently configured body? But I could not base my decision about surgery on my fears of being alone. Even if I chose not to have the surgery, Jen and I might split up anyway. Then I would regret not having surgery earlier. I knew I had to base my decisions on what I needed for me, regardless of the outcome. I am very glad that I took this view, based on how things later turned out with Jen and me.

Looking square in the face at all these implications was terrifying. To get the penis I now recognized was absent would

mean making huge sacrifices. I would have more years added to my medical transition, a lot of plans in terms of my career and study would need to be changed, and it was highly likely my relationship would end. And, to top it all off, there was no guarantee I would end up with a result I was happy with, if I was to believe all the rumours. I felt as if I was standing in the base camp of Everest with no map or climbing knowledge, with an audience yelling at me not to bother because it was far too dangerous.

Faced with all of this, I asked myself an important question: could I not just learn to love what I had down there and see it as male? I'd managed to previously, so could I not do it again? At the time, I honestly wished I could, because all of this seemed far too high a price to pay. However, the genie was out of the bottle and I couldn't put it back. Now I knew that my penis was absent, I had to move forward.

Luckily, during the decision turmoil, someone recommended that I read the book *Hung Jury*.[1] I am incredibly grateful for the recommendation because it helped enormously. Now I recommend the book to anyone who is thinking about lower surgery and needs access to honest, first-hand experiences and information. It specifically addresses the negative talk about lower surgery which was highly prevalent at the time I began my journey. It addresses many of the fears and myths around lower surgery and presents an alternative view. It made me aware for the first time that lower surgery, whilst undoubtedly a long and painful journey with risks, also had fantastic outcomes in terms of both use and aesthetics. After reading *Hung Jury*, although still unsure as to which surgery I needed, I was at least more

1 Cotten, T. (ed.) (2012) *Hung Jury: Testimonies of Genital Surgery by Transsexual Men*. Oakland, CA: Transgress Press.

confident that lower surgery could provide a result that made the sacrifices worthwhile.

When I sat down with Jen to explain how I felt, I prepared myself for the worst. I explained that I felt this choice had to be made, for the sake of my long-term mental health. If I was ever going to be free of dysphoria and feel at peace in my body, I had to address the part of me which was missing: my penis. I also let Jen know that there would be no judgement of her on my behalf if she did see this as the end of us. We agreed that, like with my journey up until then, I just had to follow what I intuitively felt my body needed. As with transition, we couldn't guess what impact a penis would have on our relationship, but at that moment we were in a good place together and so we decided we would just take it one day at a time.

After talking with Jen, there was an initial sense of relief and excitement at finally arriving at the decision that I needed to pursue lower surgery. However, this soon turned into fear, dread and utter confusion. This was because as soon as I publicly stated that I was going to go ahead with lower surgery, so many trans men came forward with horror stories about surgery. I began to see the mucky undertow of myth and misconception that surrounds lower surgery, which makes arriving at an informed choice extremely challenging.

I think one of the main reasons that lower surgery gets such a bad rap is because bad experiences generally get discussed more readily than good ones. I mean, if you are happy, you are less inclined to post on forums, aren't you? But when you have a bad experience, the drive to share it for support is much stronger. Also, people post pictures of results early in the surgical stages. This means that people see half-finished results and mistakenly think they are seeing the end product. I was just as guilty of making assumptions about lower surgery in the early days of

transition, and that contributed to my fear of lower surgery and not wanting it. The trouble is, it was much harder to stumble across positive experiences than negative ones, in all likelihood because also there were not many trans people opting for lower surgery at the time. However, this has changed hugely in the years since I began my phalloplasty journey. In fact, in the time I've been writing this, waiting lists for surgery have doubled. With more people opting for surgery, we are at least now seeing a lot more positive experiences and far more trans men are willing to educate those of us who were once naive about the process.

Despite the barrage of negativity flowing my way at the time, I held things in mind that I had learned from *Hung Jury*. Looking at lower surgery options in a new light, I began a more thorough search for information on both phallo and meta. I learnt a lot and I began to better understand the different options within the surgeries. Initially, I looked for statistics, but the issue was that there is little research into the outcome of lower surgery for trans guys. If you are reading this hoping for statistical facts, I am afraid this is the wrong book for you. I honestly found that the stats didn't help me in weighing things up anyway. What I needed was to read about the experience, how the surgery and recovery were, and what the outcome was like.

Once surgery moves from a want to a need, everything changes. Statistics become irrelevant. I always explain this in terms of having a terminal illness, and whilst this might seem like an extreme analogy, dysphoria really can be a terminal illness. The extreme distress caused by dysphoria brings up suicidal feelings for many trans people. I spent a lot of time in early transition being overwhelmed by distress to such a degree that I was exhausted and wanted the lights to go out. Therefore, if you know that you need surgery to live a pain-free life, you are going to say yes to it regardless of its complications. I now knew

that my lower dysphoria was only going to get worse. This would impact my mental health, and when my mental health suffers, I move into dangerous territory in terms of relapsing in many areas, from self-harm to problem drinking, to contemplating suicide. I had worked extremely hard on my mental health and could not let myself slip backwards. Surgery, now, was essential for me to overcome my dysphoria and live a happy life. Therefore, what mattered to me the most was not the complications but knowing that these complications could be overcome.

What I found to be of the greatest help, therefore, were the trans men who were willing to share their experiences with me. I will be forever grateful to these men because their honest sharing helped me far more than any statistical report ever did. Numbers meant nothing; I needed to know about first-hand experience of each type of surgery, and it was that which would help me to decide. These men were very honest with me and they described various degrees of complications, from very minor infections to more serious complications such as urethral strictures.[2] The men all had one thing in common. They all said that the complications had been worthwhile as they had eventually been resolved. And, after all these challenges were behind them, they had gained a wonderful penis. This was enough for me to know that the surgery was worth it.

Beginning my personal investigation in earnest now, I knew I first had to work out what my priorities were, and then I could work out which surgery would best meet those priorities. My biggest issue and source of dysphoria was using the toilet. I had by this point developed an ever-growing social dysphoria around

2 Urethral strictures are where the urethral tube narrows or completely closes, thus restricting the flow of urine. Strictures are common in phalloplasty, especially where the new urethra joins the original urethra. Though many strictures heal by themselves, often further surgeries are needed to repair the narrowed urethra tube.

accessing male bathrooms. Having to stand in a queue for what was often just one or two cubicles, compared with the many urinals, was soul-destroying. I would feel embarrassed, ashamed and like everyone was watching me. To watch every other man pee, with ease, left me feeling inadequate and emasculated. I therefore really wanted to be able to stand to pee. Using the Peecock™ device had helped me a great deal when I first started using it. My ability to go to the loo with less anxiety meant I was less anxious when out socializing. However, after the initial excitement at being able to stand to pee had worn off, using a stand-to-pee device had become frustrating. It is all too easy for them to fail and overflow, leaving you with a wet arse and an embarrassing evening. Eventually, the anxiety of using the toilet was replaced with the anxiety of a malfunctioning stand-to-pee device. I was also anxious about using it at a urinal because of the palaver in holding it a certain way so that it didn't leak. I was also worried that someone would notice that it was silicone and not flesh and I would get myself beaten up.

I remember a night out, at a gig to see Hawkwind in Oxford. I dashed to the loo at the end of the gig, trying to avoid the rush for the urinal. There were no free cubicles, just one long foreboding aluminium trough. I whipped my Peecock™ out as quickly as I could and got it into the right position. Then, before I could relax my bladder, the door opened, and in poured a troop of enormous, excessively hairy, leather-clad Hawkwind fans who surrounded me at the trough. They all whipped their penises out and started peeing. I stood, Peecock™ in hand, with a bladder that shook its head in fear and retreated. Fixing my gaze on the tarnished aluminium, my peripheral vision took in the stream of pee on both sides from men so much taller than me that these streams were near chest height. I willed myself to pee, but it just would not happen. As I stood there, the smell of urine and

leather suffocating me and adding to my rising panic, my brain went into overdrive.

'I'm just stood here holding my dick... They are going to think something is wrong with me.'

It was no good, I had to just fold my dry Peecock™ away as deftly as possible and take me and my bursting but reluctant bladder out of the room. I desperately wanted an end to these kinds of scenarios, to be able to pee normally, like any other bloke, and to not have to wait for a cubical. The ability to pee at a urinal was, therefore, my highest priority.

Being able to have penetrative sex would be good too. I realize that doesn't sound very enthusiastic, but remember, having never had penetrative sex with my own flesh, I really could not comprehend what I was missing. Therefore, I wasn't initially worried about that. Besides, as an ex-lesbian (for want of a better word), the way I had sex didn't call for much of that. Jen and I had tried to use the Peecock™ for sex, but as I said earlier, I really couldn't connect with it. There was also the issue that Jen was still identifying as a lesbian and we didn't yet know what impact a penis would have. Jen didn't know if she would want penis-in-vagina sex, which meant that having the ability to be erect might not be worthwhile.

However, just like with my decision to have lower surgery, I could not base my decisions on the type of lower surgery on what Jen wanted. As harsh as that sounds, and as much as my heart was breaking at the time at the thought of losing her, I could not deny myself the body I needed. We cannot live our lives for other people. The unhappiness and resentment that causes eats into a relationship and I knew this. Either way then, I risked losing Jen, so my best option was to choose what was right for me. I had to ask myself some honest questions and think about my long-term future. If we did split and I started dating,

would I want a penis that would function for penetrative sex? The answer to that was a resounding yes. Although I could do without it in my current relationship, I would prefer the option and choice. For those reasons, penetrative sex came second as my priority.

As well as those two priorities, I, of course, wanted to make sure I didn't lose sensation and the ability to orgasm. I also hoped that the penis would look aesthetically pleasing. From my conversations with trans people who had meta or phallo, all reported keeping sensation. They also all reported results that looked pleasing. The aesthetics were simply different in terms of size, meta appearing as a smaller, flaccid penis, and phallo as a larger, full penis. I was also incredibly grateful to these men for sharing pictures with me. Neither surgery looked anything like the Frankenstein penises described on trans forums. Both looked like a penis I would be proud to own. I felt ashamed for the times I had contributed to these rumours in the past, one of the many reasons why I now share openly too.

In better understanding both meta and phallo, and having a more balanced and realistic picture of the outcome of each, I could more easily begin to see which might be a better fit for me. I had always thought that if I ever did decide to have lower surgery, then it would only ever be metoidioplasty, and so I started my research with a bias towards that. The reason I preferred the idea of metoidioplasty was that it felt more natural – it was mainly enhancing what I had already grown myself on testosterone. I loved my T-dick, which had grown substantially. I liked that I could get an erection without the help of anything. The idea of it being freed by the process of meta, to become my own micro-penis, was extremely exciting. I also preferred the idea of meta as it wasn't as invasive as phallo and didn't leave such huge, visible scarring.

However, in identifying my priorities and revisiting my options, I was concerned that meta wouldn't provide me with what I needed. Firstly, there was my top priority of standing to pee. Although urethral hook-up was part of meta, the small size of the meta could apparently make it difficult to use a urinal. Talking with various trans guys, it seemed a mixed bag as to whether they had enough length to clear their fly. Many found they had to undo their trousers to expose most of themselves to be able to successfully use a urinal. There is no guarantee of the size you will end up with. I had about an inch of growth – substantial, but not huge – so I was not overly optimistic. I was already uncomfortable in toilets, and if I was to go through the huge upheaval of lower surgery, I wanted to be able to pee quickly, standing up at a urinal without any issues.

Then, of course, there was the issue of sex. The average size of metoidioplasty is around 4–5 centimetres. The small size means that penetrative sex is generally not possible. Some trans guys said they could manage to do it in the right position, but in general, it wasn't possible. Although penetrative sex wasn't a top priority of mine at the time, I felt it would be something I would like the option of at least. Being able to have penetrative sex might improve my dysphoria, and, if Jen was open to the idea, improve our sex life too.

With a better understanding of what I needed, I was beginning to see that metoidioplasty would likely leave me unsatisfied. To go through all that surgery, with no guarantee of being able to stand to pee or have penetrative sex, felt like taking too great a risk of feeling let down afterwards.

With meta pretty much ruled out, that left phalloplasty. Suddenly, I became aware of how much phalloplasty terrified me. I hadn't realized just how much I had been leaning towards meta, mainly out of fear of phalloplasty. The fear of phallo was

exaggerated by the bad press it received. Phallo was the surgery which I had seen so often referred to as a 'Frankenstein monster'. I knew, from the pictures that kind trans people had shared with me, that this myth was simply not true. Still, the negativity surrounding this surgery and how huge a procedure it was filled me with doubt and fear. For this reason, I began to re-evaluate my priorities and ask myself questions on how much I really needed things. Surely it would be okay to undo my trousers and pee? And for penetrative sex, I could use a sex aid to help me. I knew that the Peecock™ would work with meta and I had heard of other sex aids which were designed to work with it too.

I spent a lot of time going back and forth with this, trying to see if I could make meta work for me. After a lot of reflection, I realized that most of the compromise, if I were to have meta, would involve using my Peecock™. I would still have to wear it to help me to stand to pee and to have penetrative sex. This would, in turn, defeat the object of having lower surgery in the first place. I found myself stuck. I wanted meta, but it clearly would leave me feeling lacking, and I didn't want phalloplasty because of all the scars and the huge upheaval of the surgery. What the hell was I going to do now? Was there not a way I could just love what I had? It could be my 'mangina'. I could learn to love it. Couldn't I?

At a scheduled appointment with my gender clinic, I discussed with my therapist how stuck I was. She suggested that I make an appointment with one of the lower surgery surgeons to discuss my concerns. In the UK, we currently have one team of surgeons who all work together to perform various aspects of both types of lower surgery. This team is based in London, at St Peter's Andrology Centre. I was lucky at the time that, with waiting lists for lower surgery so short, I could easily make an appointment.

A few weeks later, I met with Mr Stephens, in London. I shared my concerns with him that metoidioplasty was too small for what I wanted, but that phalloplasty felt too invasive and I was worried about complications and scarring. He surprised me with an answer I hadn't expected. 'It is possible to create a smaller phallus,' he said. 'I can take a smaller portion of skin from your arm to leave you with less scarring.'

He explained how a smaller phallus, of around 3 inches, would give me the ability to stand to pee with ease. It might not be perfect for sex, but it could be made to work. Choosing a smaller phallus meant I would significantly reduce the risks and complications. Firstly, there would be a reduced risk with the urethral hook-up. There are often complications with urethral lengthening in phallo as there is a lot of length to reroute. A smaller phallo would mean less distance for the urethra pipe and therefore less risk of complications. Also, a smaller phallus would mean a smaller skin graft, resulting in less trauma to the arm and a less visible scar. This sounded as if it could be a perfect solution. I thanked him and said I would let him know as soon as possible. He said he could start the referral anyway, and then I could let him know which surgery type I wanted, as I progressed on the waiting list. That sounded perfect – at least I could get that ball (oh dear!) rolling whilst I worked out what exactly I wanted.

I spent a few days going over and over these choices. Although the idea of a smaller phallus seemed like it could solve some issues, on reflection I could see that it really wouldn't make that much difference. I would still have the issue with sex, and I would still have an arm scar. If I was going to have an arm scar, I might as well go with full phalloplasty rather than a smaller version.

Both meta and phallo were invasive and would take various

stages and time to complete. Both surgeries were a huge upheaval and would occupy most of my life for at least a couple of years. If I was to put myself through that, it needed to be something there was a good reason for. If I chose meta, or even just a smaller version of phallo, for me, there would be a lot of compromises, of giving up on things I wanted. It didn't feel right to go through all that and not be entirely satisfied.

I could see now, after much time in reflection, that phalloplasty was the better option for my particular needs. I would easily be able to stand to pee, and have sex. There would be no compromise involved in those two main priorities. It also made me smile when I thought about holding a full-size penis in my hand. The scarring was an issue, but there were options I could consider: tattooing, for example. At least now I knew that phalloplasty was the best option for me, to make going through such a risky and lengthy procedure worthwhile.

In being certain phalloplasty was the right choice for me, now I had the difficult choice of working out which type of phalloplasty to go for. In the UK, there are a few different methods to choose from. The most common method is radial forearm free flap phalloplasty (RFF). In RFF, a skin flap is taken from the forearm to create the penis and the urethra, in a tube inside a tube method. Because the donor flap is taken with the nerves intact, RFF statistically provides the best retention of sensation.

Other options include anterior lateral thigh pedicled flap phalloplasty (ALT), where a graft is taken from the thigh, and abdominal phalloplasty, using skin from the stomach. Both methods have the bonus of less visible scarring. However, both also have a lower outcome of erotic and tactile sensation and often have urethral hook-up complications. The outcome of any of these surgeries is also greatly affected by your size and amount of body fat.

I completely ruled out abdominal phalloplasty as it is rarely done with urethral hook-up. Also, I didn't like the fact that there would be a seam scar running along the top length of my penis. I briefly considered ALT as I liked the idea of not having a visible scar. Sensation with ALT came a close second to RFF, with lots of guys saying that they could still orgasm using their buried clitoris (I'll explain that shortly). However, I have huge thighs, and this would have resulted in a very thick penis, needing to be trimmed down at a later stage. Additionally, my body size would have increased the chance of urethral hook-up complications, due to the excess fat on my thighs.

With my absolute top priority being the ability to stand to pee, it was clear that RFF provided the highest chance of a good outcome in that area. Aesthetically, RFF looked to be the best result for my body-size type. The use of nerves from the forearm also meant the greatest chance of retaining both erotic and tactile sensation. It certainly looked as though radial forearm phalloplasty would be the right decision for me.

Making Sacrifices for a Penis

Weighing Up the Losses and Gains in Phalloplasty

Now I was sure I wanted lower surgery and that RFF phalloplasty was the best option. Hurrah! At least that was one giant weight off my shoulders. However, that was only the beginning of my decision-making. There was still so much more to consider. Each type of lower surgery has many other choices within it. As well as having to decide on which skin donor site you want to use, there are also various other choices you need to make. For example, whether to have a hysterectomy, a vaginectomy, and whether to bury your clitoris. Making all these tough decisions is no easy task.

Someone who is not familiar with being trans or not understanding trans lives might think that if you want a penis, why would you want to keep your vagina and clitoris? Well, unfortunately, it isn't that straightforward. The reason is that these seemingly simple decisions carry with them a lot of huge implications, in terms of sensation outcome. It's not so much that we want to keep these female parts, you see – at least, that wasn't the case for me, but rather that I wanted to keep the ability to feel pleasure. Sacrificing the vagina and clitoris meant

losing the sensation and pleasure from these areas, and, in turn, risking that a newly configured genital area might not produce the same sensation.

I knew I wanted a penis. I wanted that newly configured genital area, but the fear of the worst-case scenario of losing sensation and the ability to orgasm was terrifying. If I could have had an absolute guarantee of keeping sensation, then I wouldn't have hesitated. I wasn't attached to those parts in any way, but I was attached to feeling sexual pleasure, especially now that I had a sex drive for the first time. Dysphoria is complex. It often isn't one entity but exists in various parts and in varying degrees. My chest dysphoria, for example, was much more straightforward in many ways. I couldn't look at my chest, I couldn't have people touch it, and even just knowing those alien lumps were squashed under a binder made my insides crawl. My lower dysphoria, however, was entirely different. Looking at my naked body by this point was hugely distressing. My lack of a penis was now a source of mental dysphoria in how I looked, and social dysphoria in affecting the spaces I could access. However, my physical dysphoria, in having my genitals touched, was more manageable. As long as I touched myself in a certain way, using my T-dick rather than my vagina, I could still experience pleasure. In many ways, had my lower dysphoria been as intense and all-encompassing as my chest dysphoria had been, my decision-making may have been easier. As it was, in being able to still get some pleasure from my body, choosing whether or not to have the vaginectomy, and choosing whether or not to bury my T-dick, felt like such a difficult choice to make.

The vaginectomy was the hardest decision for me. I rarely used what I affectionately called my Batcave, but the idea of it being closed, for good, terrified me. What if I suddenly missed the option of penetration? What if it was like a phantom limb,

an itch that could never again be scratched? What if my new penis didn't bring me sexual pleasure? Then I'd have no way to enjoy myself. It all felt just too final. I understood that most people wanted the vagina gone in order to be rid of any 'female attributes'. I started to feel a bit 'not trans enough' when these concerns came up for me. Did the fact that my dysphoria wasn't intense and that I was considering keeping some 'female' parts invalidate my need for surgery?

I know, from speaking to other trans people, that I was not alone in feeling like this. I think it's completely understandable to worry and it is important to talk about it. There is the risk that a vaginectomy could change the way you feel pleasure, and you may be someone who likes internal stimulation. I liked the outskirts of my Batcave but not the inner cavern (so to speak). I worried that if I opted for a vaginectomy, I would lose the ability to feel pleasure, and then regret the procedure. Having these worries does not mean you aren't 'trans enough' to have surgery. These are our bodies, and even if parts of them cause distress, it is still a frightening prospect to have them changed irreversibly. I think it's a wise person who first works their way through these difficult and complex feelings before having surgery.

Here in the UK, the London team do not offer a total vaginectomy, where the entire vagina is removed. The reasoning is because it is seen to be a risky surgery that can cause significant bleeding. Instead, they perform a partial vaginectomy, which removes just the vagina lining, using electrocautery. Over time, the raw walls inside the vagina stick to each other, thus closing the vaginal space.

I discussed my vaginectomy concerns with Mr Stephens. Apparently, the main reason the vaginectomy is suggested is that it is the best option to prevent cancer. Once the scrotum is created, access to the vagina is made more difficult and the

entrance will be tighter, making it hard to have smear tests. This could then mean that early cancer signs are missed. Keeping the vagina can also make the urethral hook-up part more complicated. However, Mr Stephens told me that some trans guys do keep their vagina. The best option, if I wanted to keep it, would be to not have the scrotoplasty, so that access to the vagina was easier. However, without scrotoplasty the pump erectile device would not be possible, as the pump for the device goes in one testicle. Instead, I could have the semi-rigid rod, which would just be bent to shape and thus not need a pump.

Once again, I was back to having to have a modified penis option. If I wanted to keep my Batcave, and with it some guarantee of retaining the ability to feel pleasure, then I would have to sacrifice having testicles. This would leave me with a strange-looking penis, with an opening underneath. I now knew that I wanted a full-size penis, as close to a naturally grown one as possible. Keeping my Batcave would get in the way of that, but the other option – to have it gone – just seemed too great a risk to me.

Choosing whether to bury my T-dick was another excruciatingly difficult choice. Despite my lower dysphoria, one thing I did like about my genitals was my T-dick. This might sound daft to anyone who isn't trans, but I was immensely proud of the mini-penis I had grown. And, with the arrival of my sex drive, it was a source of great pleasure. So, having to say goodbye to my own-grown creation was painfully difficult.

Whatever choice I made, it would dramatically alter the appearance of my T-dick. When you choose to have it buried, it is stripped back, and a thin layer of skin closed over the top. If it's left unburied, it is stripped back but is still accessible, hidden under the penis and slightly behind the scrotum.

Mr Stephens had told me that choosing whether to bury my

T-dick or not wouldn't impact my surgery at all. He said that it made no odds either way. Burial or non-burial was purely a choice based on aesthetics – in how you wanted things to look. Of course, there were implications for sensation and orgasm too. Leaving the T-dick unburied would mean I could still directly access it for stimulation should I want to. Burying my T-dick would make it harder to access. However, speaking with other trans guys, I had been told it is still easy to find and stimulate, even under the skin.

The thing I was the most scared about was losing sensation and the ability to orgasm. I had only just found my sex drive after years of feeling about as alive as a week-old lettuce leaf. The thought of not being able to feel pleasure, now that I knew what it was, terrified me. As with all the research I had attempted to do, trying to find useful statistics on sensation outcome was almost impossible. The few trans guys I had spoken to reported different degrees of sensation but all were satisfied and able to orgasm. Although I did feel slightly reassured by that, what if I was that rare one that lost all ability to feel sexual arousal and orgasm?

To go through all the surgery and to be left with a penis I was unable to feel pleasure with would be intolerable. Just the thought of it was enough to knock the wind out of me. For this reason, I did initially think that the most sensible option would be to leave my T-dick unburied. That way, should I not have sensation in my new penis, I could at least easily access my T-dick. Burying it seemed too much of an additional risk to me.

However, I didn't particularly want something sticking out from under my penis. Even if my T-dick was hidden, when I or a partner played with my new penis, they would be able to feel it or see it. I wanted an aesthetically pleasing penis. Having a random nubbin sticking out interfered with that. Therefore, neither

option was a perfect solution. Either option would involve a loss. It was just a matter of which loss I could live with, for the benefit of gaining a full-size penis.

These agonizing decisions are what make choosing lower surgery incredibly different from choosing top surgery. In many ways, top surgery is a relatively easy choice, in that top surgery is straightforward and the outcome is well known. Also, in comparison, the risks are relatively low for top surgery, whereas lower surgery, because of the hugely invasive nature and the various affected areas, has so much that can go wrong. As you can see from these huge and difficult choices, though, what sets lower surgery apart more than anything is that it is a surgery of compromise. It is impossible to get a penis without first making many difficult sacrifices.

In making these decisions, then, I found that I had to spend a great deal of time weighing up the many losses and gains in going ahead with phalloplasty. These compromises aren't just about sensation either – there are many other losses to process.

One of the biggest losses to deal with is the loss of a scar-free body. I knew that choosing RFF phalloplasty would mean sacrificing my forearm. A large piece of skin, from the wrist to halfway up the arm and almost all the way around the arm, would be taken. Even if I healed exceptionally well, there would never be any way of hiding this scar other than to keep it covered. I could choose to have it tattooed once healed, but regardless, my forearm would never be the same again. The visible scarring is why I and many other trans guys are so hesitant to have RFF phalloplasty.

I had huge concerns about how I would feel about the arm scar. I have a history of self-harm – the entire length of both my arms is covered in scars. These scars have now faded and I have come to terms with them. But the thought of having a new

and obvious scar was not one I relished. There is also the risk of permanent damage being done to the arm, which, although rare, does happen.

It's not just the arm, either. There would be two giant scars under my buttocks where they would take the skin to replace the skin on my forearm. Also, there would be more scarring across the top of my pubic area, from where they would attach the new nerves and artery. My body would be significantly impacted and would never be the same again. I do heal well, but you can never know for sure how well your scars will heal.

Another huge loss to process would be the loss of fertility. Having a hysterectomy, as part of my phalloplasty surgery, would mean I would be unable to have my own children. I have gone back and forth on wanting children over the years. When I was younger, I was adamant that I didn't want children. However, after having top surgery, I soon noticed that my feelings about children were changing. I think perhaps my earlier reasons for not wanting children were more about me not wanting to go through childbirth and be the mum. In becoming confident in my male identity, I now see my role as paternal. From that perspective I really wanted to be a dad. In fact, I still do.

I did explore options for storing my eggs when I first began my transition. However, as much as I would have liked to have had biological children, I felt that as I was approaching 40, storing eggs was not a viable option for me. My age was against me in how many eggs I would produce. Also, approaching transition so late in life, I didn't want to waste any more time. Egg harvesting can take a year or so, and at the time I transitioned it was not available on our National Health Service. I knew it wasn't an option for me, and neither was retaining my womb and getting pregnant at a later date. There was no way I could have coped with being pregnant – that would have been a hugely

dysphoria-inducing event for me. I had, therefore, already spent a great deal of time processing the loss of ever having a biological child of my own. But still, a hysterectomy was a huge final loss to process.

I was, however, quite glad to see the back of my female reproductive organs, because they had been causing me a great deal of pain. From around a year on testosterone, I kept having excruciating stomach cramps which felt very much like period pains. Every time I had the pain, I feared I was about to start bleeding. I didn't start bleeding, but the fear remained.

I have been led to believe that there are two main reasons why some trans guys get this pain. The first is that testosterone causes the internal parts (ovaries, womb, etc.) to atrophy. Then, as muscle mass increases on testosterone, the contractions from these internal parts are felt more strongly and hence cause more pain. The shrivelling up and cramping of these organs can often lead to more pain for trans guys, and that is certainly what happened to me. I wanted it all out ASAP!

Most professionals do suggest that trans guys should have a hysterectomy after being on testosterone for a few years, not only because of pain but because of a higher risk of cancer. Like with the vaginectomy, the cancer risk is to do with trans guys (understandably) not wanting to have smear tests, so early cancer signs are missed. Therefore, removing the womb, uterus and ovaries reduces the risk of cancer developing in the first place.

I was looking forward to having all traces of my female reproductive organs gone, in the hope that the phantom period pains would disappear. However, there was, of course, some sadness with the realization that this would forever draw a line under my ability to have biological children.

With all of these incredibly difficult decisions to make, it's possible to see why so many trans people choose not to have

lower surgery. There is a huge element of risk involved with the decisions you make, and no absolute guarantees. The trouble is, there are not an awful lot of reliable statistics regarding lower surgery, and even fewer on the long-term implications of having it done. It is still relatively early days with these surgical procedures, though, and was especially so when I began my journey. Phalloplasty is very young in the UK (the London team at St Peter's only began using that technique in 1997).

As I mentioned previously, though, statistics didn't really tell me anything. In every decision I wrestled with, I relied upon word-of-mouth experiences from guys who had gone through it themselves. These stories were what I really needed to hear. I knew, based both on the sketchy statistics I had read and on the invasive nature of the surgery, that there were bound to be problems along the way. The only thing in question would be how big that complication might be. Therefore, hearing from guys who had overcome the difficult times and had no regrets reassured me that this surgery was worth all the pain and upheaval.

Making all these decisions, then, was a case of taking a chunk of time to really think about the losses and gains of RFF phalloplasty and the various decisions within the surgical process. I had to be brutally honest with myself about what I was willing to sacrifice to get the penis I wanted. This was not going to be a 'have your cake and eat it' type of surgery. Every single decision I made would have huge implications for my health and my sexual future. I also knew I had to carefully manage my expectations of what phalloplasty would give me. I had to accept the fact that a phalloplasty would be close to, but never quite match, a biologically grown penis. Only if I could accept these risks and these realistic outcomes, could I even think of going ahead.

After reflecting on all the risks and potential losses, I was

still sure that RFF was the right type of phalloplasty for me. Of all the other phalloplasty types, RFF came the closest to how I visualized my penis. I felt 100 per cent sure that, for me, accepting further scarring on my arms was worth it to create a penis that looked pleasing. The fact that RFF also seemed to give the best chance of a good sensation outcome also made sacrificing my forearm worthwhile.

I still was not sure about the vaginectomy and burial of my T-dick. However, those procedures wouldn't be done until a later stage. Here in the UK, at the time I had my surgery, both the vaginectomy and burial were done in stage two. At least this gave me a little longer to decide, and I hoped that once I had my penis created in stage one, I might feel more certain. A lot of my transition needs have only become apparent by stepping forward. I hoped that the same would be the case with decisions within phalloplasty. At least I now knew enough and was certain enough to proceed with stage one. I had done all I could do, for now. I just had to wait for my next appointment with my doctor at my gender clinic. I could then ask for the official referral process to begin.

Preparing for a Penis

The Official Referral and a Long Wait

Having finally arrived at a decision I felt sure of, I began to feel excited about phalloplasty. I had a pre-arranged appointment with Dr Nicholson at my gender identity clinic in the August of 2014 and was very keen to see him and get the ball rolling.

Dr Nicholson knew that I had been mulling over the decision, because I had expressed doubts at my previous appointment. He had been very supportive of allowing me time to go away and work through my concerns to arrive at a decision. I am very grateful to my clinic for not rushing me in this decision or pressuring me in any way to decide more quickly than I was able to. I also had lots of help to work things through with my therapist at the clinic. I know that without a doubt, taking a year to thoroughly explore lower surgery and make sure I was choosing what was right for me helped enormously in managing my surgical journey.

On the day of the appointment with Dr Nicholson, my heart was in my mouth. I was scared now that, having taken so much time, I might be told I couldn't have phalloplasty as I hadn't been sure enough. Of course, this wasn't the case at all – clinics want

you to be sure and do not penalize you on the time it takes you to arrive at a decision.

'Finlay Games?'

The sound of my name startled me out of my daydreams. I pushed myself out of my chair and headed into Dr Nicholson's office, taking a seat opposite him across a large table. He looked up at me and smiled warmly. I took a deep breath and without pause, poured out my desire to have radial forearm phalloplasty. Saying the words out loud felt liberating, exhilarating and terrifying all at once.

He didn't even hesitate to agree with my decision. By this point, we had met on numerous occasions. Plus, having regular meetings with my therapist at the Laurels Clinic, it would have been clear that I had worked hard on working through my decisions. He read out the notes from my case file, saying how clearly my progression showed that I was taking the right path and that he was very happy to sign off on my having phalloplasty.

At the time I began my lower surgery journey, the procedure, as required by the NHS system, was that after a referral from my clinic doctor (in my case Dr Nicholson), I then had to gain a second, independent opinion from a psychiatrist before being officially referred for surgery. The purpose of this was to obtain an unbiased opinion from a person who was not involved with my current treatment. The independent doctor would examine my history, review my gender journey, and question me on my thoughts regarding lower surgery. Then, if the independent psychiatrist agreed with Dr Nicholson regarding my suitability for phalloplasty, the official referral would go ahead. This would involve the two doctors (the gender clinic doctor and the independent psychiatrist) signing their agreement and then sending it to the surgical team at St Peter's. This process would

allow funding to be generated so that I could be put on the list for the first stage of my phalloplasty.

The referral process is such an archaic system. Even though being trans is no longer listed as a mental health diagnosis, the system is still very much pathologized and psychiatric assessments are needed at various points along the road. I take deep breaths, suck it up and hope to see an end to this system and a better one in the near future – but that's likely a topic for a completely different book, so I'll stop there and get off my soapbox.

Dr Nicholson arranged an appointment with a psychiatrist called Dr Williams. I worried this might take a long time, but I was relieved to receive an appointment for the following November. I did, however, feel concerned about seeing someone new. I worried that, not knowing me, he might see my mental health history and decide I was a bad candidate.

I have a very turbulent mental health past, which really is unsurprising, considering I spent half my life not knowing I was trans. Depression, anxiety, self-harm, addiction and personality disorder make for a very thick medical file. I'd had the same concerns when I first began my gender transition that my mental health history might negatively affect my access to gender services, hormones and surgery. However, my gender clinic was very firm in its statement that mental health problems do not halt transition. The therapists I saw at the Laurels Clinic understood that many trans people present with mental health issues, due to the distress of gender dysphoria. The only time mental health issues would be a concern was if they were not well managed.

By the time I started my gender transition, my mental health issues were still very prevalent but also very well managed. I regularly attended Alcoholics Anonymous (AA) meetings to maintain my abstinence from alcohol and weed. By working through the AA programme and having counselling support, I

was better managing my anxiety. I no longer self-harmed and had instead learned healthy ways to manage my fluctuating moods and high anxiety. However, as much as my mental health was managed and I had the support of my therapists, I worried whether an independent psychiatrist would feel differently.

I needn't have worried. Dr Williams turned out to be a surprisingly nice guy – in fact, the nicest psychiatrist I have ever had the pleasure to meet (and I have met a lot in my time). It was nothing like I imagined. I had been worried that, with his being a stranger to me, I would have to work hard to prove my need for a penis and suitability for surgery. But of course, he had already spoken with Dr Nicholson and was already familiar with my case. Instead, he just wanted to get a sense of who I was and make sure for himself that I was suitable for surgery.

After a general chat about life and transition, he said I was a surgeon's dream: fit, healthy, non-smoking, non-drinking and very clear in what I wanted. He declared that he was very happy to agree with Dr Nicholson's recommendation for me to go ahead with phalloplasty. I had to contain my excited seal-clapping and refrain from throwing my arms around him in relief. Now that both doctors were in agreement about my suitability for surgery, the official referral would be sent from my clinic to St Peter's Andrology. Once this letter was received, I would then be sent a letter for an official appointment which would serve as my pre-consultation for the first stage. Bring it on!

However, as with every step in the gender transition process, nothing happens quickly. Managing this incredibly stressful waiting time is not easy at all, especially when you have crippling gender dysphoria and mental health challenges. A huge part of this journey, whether you have pre-existing mental health challenges or not, is to learn how to look after your mental wellbeing. I took advantage of every kind of therapy and support I could get

to manage the waiting times. As well as having support from my gender clinic therapist, I also had sessions with a local counsellor. Many charities and local clinics run counselling sessions and I highly recommend seeking these out. Trans support groups, either face to face or virtual, are a lifesaver in this journey too. The support of people who 'get' it, and have been where you are, helps enormously. I have also learned to fill my time with small, achievable goals to break down the waiting times. So, whilst I awaited the phone call for the official pre-op consultation with St Peter's, I looked at what else I could do in the meantime to prepare myself.

One thing I could do to prepare was to investigate hair removal options. I was understandably concerned about having a hairy penis. Who wouldn't be concerned by that? My arms are covered in thick, dark hair and so I knew if I did nothing, my new penis would have a comb-over. Hair removal is expensive. At the time I had my surgery, the NHS funding didn't cover hair removal, unless the surgeon said you needed it. To explain, the underside of your forearm is the skin they use for the urethra. It is very important that the underside isn't hairy, as hair in the urethra can cause complications down the line. A hairy urethra can lead to urine infections, strictures, and potentially cause the entire hook-up to fail. Therefore, the surgeons will only recommend you for hair removal if the underside of your arms are hairy. If the underside isn't deemed to be too hairy, they won't approve funding for hair removal as it is then considered to only be cosmetic. I personally think this is ridiculously unfair. In trying to cure dysphoria with lower surgery, are we not looking for the best outcome? Is not wanting a hairy penis cosmetic? I think this ruling is now beginning to change and I have seen a few people manage to secure a bit of funding for hair removal.

At the time of my own surgery, I was worried that I did not

have enough hair on the underside of my arms to be approved for funding. However, just before I saw Dr Nicholson that August, my therapist at the gender clinic felt able to refer me so that I could get a head start on hair removal.

The referral for hair removal was quick in comparison with everything else. A month later, I received a letter, detailing that I would receive funding for six sessions of laser hair removal. I rang to organize my first session in September of 2014 at Bristol's Frenchay Hospital. The first appointment was to trial a test area to see how my skin and hair took to it.

Let me tell you now that laser hair removal is bloody painful. It's like a prickly, hot electric shock. The longer the nurse kept the laser on, the more it increased the pain, but in short bursts it was more manageable. The good news is that it is over quickly. After the first session, my arm was sore and pink; but a few hours later, the colour returned to normal and the soreness disappeared.

The nurse said that I needed to lose some of my tan for the laser removal to work effectively. However, she was also optimistic that in the time frame I estimated I had before the first stage, they should be able to at least minimize the amount of hair. Success would depend on how my hair reacted to the laser treatment over time. Some people are lucky, and find that their hair dies quickly, whereas others find their hair is more resilient. I was booked to come back in a month's time and was told that I needed to keep that part of my arm covered so that the tan would fade.

The strangest thing about having hair removal was that it really brought home to me the fact that I was going ahead with surgery. It was the initial moment when I was beginning to change my body, perhaps only in a small and not irreversible way, and yet it was a momentous occasion as it was the sign of things to come.

Not long after starting laser therapy, around December, 2014, at last a letter arrived from my gender clinic. I was nervous opening it, fearing it would tell me they had changed their minds. What if, now that I'd started having this laser hair removal, they'd changed their minds about referring me for surgery? I know I am not alone with feeling this way during gender transition. It's so hard to get anywhere that we fear it'll be taken away at every step.

The letter was a copy of my official referral, confirming that the referral had been made. When this happens, they send out two letters: one for you and one for the surgical team. Once the surgical team has the letter, they can put you on a list for a consultation and then the wheels are set in motion waiting for stage one phalloplasty. So, on opening the envelope and finding the magical letter, I immediately rang St Peter's to ask if they had also received a copy. The secretary I spoke to confirmed that they had received it and could offer me a consultation appointment in the New Year. This time, I would be seeing Mr Henry, one of the three consultant surgeons at St Peter's Andrology in London at the time. This would be to finalize everything and put me on a waiting list for stage one. Finally, it was happening. Excitedly, I shared my news with Jen, who didn't react well at all. I had worried that at some point, when the reality of a penis joining our relationship hit, things might start to go wrong. However, her reaction turned out to have nothing to do with my penis at all.

Not long after I had my top surgery, Jen admitted to me that she had been struggling with her identity. At the time, I thought (or hoped) that this was more about my new male identity rocking her lesbian identity and that it would settle down as we both adjusted. However, Jen had now realized that she was transgender as well, and that she too wanted to go through transition.

I felt devastated, and guilty for feeling devastated. I also felt very selfish for being so resistant to this news, but I didn't want to be gay. I was only just making sense of the man I was, and as far as I was concerned, I was a straight man. After years of living as a gay woman and having to be careful showing affection in public, it had been wonderful to finally be a straight couple and not have that worry. My fears were that, as two gay men, we would be even less safe. Then, of course, there were my hopes for what my penis might do for improving our sex life. Now that Jen was going to live as male, would that mean yet another barrier to sex? Would Jen want penetrative sex once she was living as a man?

I felt obligated to support Jen and felt guilty for feeling obligated. Jen had managed to overcome her own identity confusion and stay with me when I came out and I wanted to do the same for her. I was in no doubt that I loved her. Perhaps, over time, love would be enough and it would work itself out. I wanted to at least try.

By the New Year, Jen had begun to live permanently as Alex. I was adjusting to the name and pronoun change and we were working through things. In many ways, my initial worry about how Alex might react to my penis was still the same. In Alex's previous identity as a lesbian, I had concerns about whether penetrative sex would be something that Alex would want. And now I had the same concerns because, as a man, he might, understandably, have too much dysphoria for penetrative sex using his vagina. At the time, I was adamantly against the idea of anal sex. However, that would change in unexpected ways as my transition progressed, which I will elaborate on later. Either way, I had made peace with the fact that I might end up with a partner and not have the ability to use my penis to penetrate. This wasn't new, so in many ways nothing had changed. I

would just have to deal with that when it came up. For the time being, I just focused on the goal ahead: my first appointment at St Peter's.

The New Year finally arrived, and I began to prepare for my first official appointment at St Peter's Andrology. The appointment would be an assessment, and if everything was okay, I would be placed on the list for my first stage of phalloplasty. My appointment was with Mr Henry at Highgate Private Hospital in London. The surgeons work at a few different hospitals in London, so appointment venues could often vary.

I wasn't sure what to expect at my first consultation. I had the usual fear that for one reason or another they would change their minds or there would be something wrong with me, meaning they wouldn't do the surgery. At every official appointment, I always imagined them telling me I wasn't 'trans enough' or suitable enough for surgery. This is one of the hardest things about transition: feeling at the mercy of everyone else's decisions on the most important aspects of your life. It's impossible to relax on this journey. Each time a stage in the medical journey was complete, I would sigh with relief – no more performing for a while (because it does feel as if you are a circus monkey jumping through fiery hoops). Then another stage would approach and yet again I would be paraded in front of experts who got to decide if what I was requesting was what I needed. It's really disempowering, and it feels so insecure, like at any moment, all your options could be taken away. To survive this journey, especially the lower surgery one, you need a ton of resilience and ability to see the positive to keep you upbeat.

Despite my anxiety, the appointment went well. There were no questions about why I wanted surgery because that wasn't his job. I had already been assessed and so there was no need to go over my suitability for surgery. This was such a relief.

The entire focus was instead on the details of the surgery and assessing my medical suitability for phalloplasty. Mr Henry was a lovely man; I actually felt more at ease with him than with Mr Stephens, in terms of conversation. Mr Henry went over my consultation letters, checking my history and details and confirming that we were on the same page with my desires for surgery. He checked the suitability of my arm for RFF phallo. It was important that I had good blood flow in the arm as veins would be harvested in the first stage to provide blood flow to my new penis. I was reassured that there were no issues with that. My skin also needed to be in good condition in order to be grafted. I had been concerned about the scarring on my arm from my years of self-harming (I have scars covering the entire length of my forearms and the ones around my wrists are particularly bad). Mr Henry said that the scars on my arm were not deep, so shouldn't cause any issues. The scars around my wrists, however, were much deeper. As the skin on my wrist would be the tip of my penis, Mr Henry said that they would likely extend the graft up a few more centimetres towards my elbow, to avoid compromising the tip. It was a relief to know that the scars wouldn't prevent me having RFF.

In the earlier, non-official appointment, which I'd had with Mr Stephens, he had suggested putting on half a stone in order to have more fat on my arm. I really couldn't see how this could work, but I did it anyway, because it is always best to do what your surgeon tells you. At the consultation with Mr Henry, he said nothing about my weight gain. He certainly didn't say the arm was skinny or anything and I really don't know if it made any difference. At the end of my journey now, my penis is of good girth, both when flaccid and erect, so I really can't see if that half stone made any impact.

I asked more questions about T-dick placement; I had found

information that suggested that burying it may cause issues with the urethral hook-up. Mr Henry said it wouldn't cause any issues. He stressed that burial was more about aesthetics and whether or not I wanted to be able to access my T-dick post-surgery. I still was no closer to a decision, but I was reminded that it was okay. I could see how I felt after stage one and decide from there.

Our appointment lasted about half an hour. At the end, Mr Henry concluded that he was happy to go ahead and that it would likely be him or Mr Stephens doing my stage one procedure. The team (at the time of my surgery) consisted of three main surgeons: Mr Stephens, Mr Henry and Mr Bruno. I asked if I could choose a surgeon and he said that I could but that it might increase the waiting time due to the surgeon's availability. I was told that most people don't request anyone specific because each surgeon is equally skilled. This is very different to top surgery and it feels strange to have little say in who performs surgery on you. I would like to see a future where we have more surgeons and more informed choice because, surely, like with top surgery, some are more skilled with certain body sizes than others?

I asked about surgery waiting times. Mr Henry said I would likely have first stage phalloplasty in the following April, 2015, due to the increase in the number of surgeries they were performing, and funding requirements. I could also be put on a cancellation list if I could be available at short notice. I said that I was happy to receive short notice – anything to get a date as quickly as possible. I was lucky in that my life was flexible, my work was voluntary and my studies were via distance-learning.

I also asked Mr Henry if he knew which hospital I would likely attend. When I had my surgery, three hospitals were in use. They were Highgate Private Hospital and St John & St Elizabeth Hospital (both in London) and Spire Thames Valley Hospital in Slough. However, I was informed that where the procedure

takes place depends on the date and which surgeon is available. Choosing a specific hospital was, therefore, rather difficult and rarely happened. This was unfortunate because I wanted to be able to choose a hospital that had good feedback from trans people. However, I went on to discover that by and large, hospital experience was subjective and far more down to each individual's experience than anything else. Whilst some trans people had great experiences at one hospital, others did not.

Regardless, I personally found this lack of choice hard to manage. Not knowing who would be performing my surgery or where it would take place caused huge levels of uncertainty and anxiety. The lack of choice also felt disempowering, especially when comparing it with my top surgery experience where I had full control over the choice of surgeon and location. I am someone who likes to be informed and involved, so a huge part of this process involved learning to manage the lack of personal control.

At least I was on the waiting list. Now, all I could do was wait to receive a letter or a phone call, giving me a date for surgery. Once again, the process of waiting began. Waiting lists were about three months long when I started my journey. At the time of writing this, waiting lists are growing rapidly. I don't think it's an over-exaggeration to say that gender services are in crisis. More people are coming out and choosing to medically transition. More trans men are now choosing lower surgery, whereas at one time few trans men did. This stands as a testament to how much lower surgeries have improved. However, here in the UK, we do not have the capacity to meet these rising numbers. Currently, the surgical team at St Peter's is our only lower surgery option and there are only a handful of surgeons there. This means that services are over-saturated and under-resourced. Choosing to go private is not an option for most trans people, as the average cost for phalloplasty in the UK is currently £50,000.

The wait for surgery is also very difficult to manage because, unlike with top surgery, you are often not given a date in advance. Instead, it is not uncommon to receive a surgery date with only a week's notice. I expect this is to try to get people through their surgeries as timely as possible, so rather than set dates, they fill slots and cancellations as they arise.

The combination of long waiting lists and short notice made me feel like I was in constant anxiety mode. The frustration of not knowing when surgery might happen, but also knowing I could get a call out of the blue, was incredibly stressful. Being at the mercy of a medical establishment is disempowering and soul-destroying. Therefore, this journey requires you to learn ways to look after your mental wellbeing to avoid becoming overly stressed. As I mentioned earlier, seeking out as much support as you can, from professionals and peers, is vital.

I did my best to continue with my life whilst I waited for a date. However, three months went by, April arrived and still I hadn't received a date. I rang St Peter's to ask for an update and was advised I could expect something in the next six to eight weeks. This would mean surgery might not take place until May or possibly June. Although my study life was flexible, my exams were set and would be taking place in June. I knew it would not be sensible to have surgery too close to my exams. It would not do my exam results or my surgery recovery any good. After an agonizing back and forth with myself, I felt I had no choice but to put surgery off until I had finished my exams.

Postponing surgery was a hard decision, especially after waiting so long already. Being an older guy, I had the distinct feeling of lack of time. I wanted surgery done as soon as possible, so I would have time left in my life to enjoy my new penis. Additionally, I worried about my body and its ability to cope – the

older I got, the harder the toll on my body from surgery would be. However, there was nothing I could do. My exams were set and that had to be my priority for now. Stage one was to be the most recovery-intensive and so I knew having a good chunk of free time to heal without any pressure was sensible. I rang St Peter's to explain and asked to be taken off the cancellation list for now and to be considered for a date later in the year.

I decided to use the additional waiting time productively and have more laser hair removal. Six sessions later and my arms were significantly less hairy and the hair that was there was much finer. However, six sessions were not enough really. In hindsight, I should have started hair removal a lot sooner and paid for extra sessions out of my own pocket. Most of the research says that for super-hairy guys like me, whether you choose electrolysis or laser hair removal, you really need to do a year's worth of sessions to get hair-free or as close to it as possible. For the purpose of my surgery, the important underside part was hair-free, but the rest was in need of much more work.

Summer came, and with it my exams. Still no date for surgery. Then, when it was beginning to feel like it might never happen, on the 11th August, 2015, I received the phone call I had been longing for. A couple of my best friends, Ryan and Lucy, were visiting Oxford and I was so busy chatting I didn't hear my phone ring. I checked the voicemail.

'Oh, my word,' I blurted. 'That was a call from London!'

'Ring them back now!' Ryan insisted, his wide grin matching my rising joy.

I pressed number five on my keypad to redial, my heart in my mouth, with Ryan and Lucy staring at me now, a pair of giant toothy grins.

'St Peter's Andrology?', declared an efficient-sounding female voice.

I asked to talk to David, who at the time oversaw surgery dates.

'Hey, Finn, there is a cancellation for the 24th August if you are available?'

I spluttered my yes and my appreciation as David read out the finer details. I was to be admitted to Spire Thames Valley Hospital on Sunday the 23rd August at 6 pm, with my surgery to take place the following day. That was just under two weeks away. Oh, my goodness!

I put down the phone and conveyed the news to an equally thrilled Ryan and Lucy. As I said the words out loud, relief cascaded down through my body as a hot wave of nervousness made its way up and met it in the middle.

It's such a strange thing to explain to anyone outside the trans community how, on the one hand, there is huge nervousness about surgery but, on the other hand, also huge excitement. These contradictory feelings can be very difficult to balance. Talking about these conflicting emotions is difficult too because you fear it calls your readiness for surgery into question. Telling people who are not transgender and who do not understand trans lives that you are scared can often be met with a 'Well, why are you choosing to have surgery then?'

When other people question us, it can be all too easy then to start questioning ourselves.

'If I am nervous, does this mean surgery isn't right for me?'

Let me tell you that it is very healthy to have fears and very unhealthy to not talk about them. It's surgery. It's painful. The recovery time is long. You can't know the outcome or if you will have any complications. Of course, you are scared. Who wouldn't be scared to have surgery? It is okay and normal to have both fear and excitement. It's about learning how to hold them both in the same space and finding people whom you can share that with.

I knew I was not in any doubt at all about having phalloplasty. I had taken a good chunk of time to research and mull things over. I knew the risks and I knew what I wanted. Best of all, I knew I was in the right place and time to have this surgery done. As hard as it had been to ask for a later date, I had made the right decision to postpone surgery. With my exams out of the way, I had completed my study module and didn't start the next one until October. This would give me a clear chunk of time to concentrate on my healing. It's funny how things often happen just as they need to. I have followed my instincts a lot on this journey and they have never failed me.

Not long after getting my surgery date, I was walking through Jericho in Oxford one day, mulling over the strange mix of emotions I felt. I bumped into Elizabeth, a female friend who was aware that I was soon to have my surgery and who was pregnant. We were discussing how hard I was finding it to deal with excitement and fear both battling for space in my head.

'You know what?', Elizabeth exclaimed with a tilt of her head, 'That sounds a lot like childbirth! You want this beautiful being which you are about to bring into life, but, at the same time, the outcome is unknown. What will the baby look like? Will you bond? How will your life change? How will it change the relationship with yourself and significant others? And there has to be a lot of pain to go through first to get this beautiful thing.'

I stared at Elizabeth in shock. 'Oh, my goodness, you are so right!'

Elizabeth added how she was scared that after the birthing experience her body would be forever changed, '...in a beautiful way, of course, but I will still have to adjust and get to know my body all over again.'

Never in a million years did I expect to be having a conversation with someone about the similarities between childbirth

and phalloplasty, but my friend was right. I was about to have a brand-new penis; my body would be forever changed. My new body would change my relationship dynamic. Talking with Elizabeth and seeing the complexity of the situation really helped me to embrace both conflicting emotions and find space for them to live together in my head. They were both valid and part of the process of birthing my new penis.

Feeling much more able to manage the intensity of the pre-surgery emotions, I spent the next couple of weeks occupying myself with buying various recovery supplies. If it looked helpful, I bought it. Dressings, pillows, vitamins, etc. I've learned in this journey that you can never have too many medical supplies. I also made sure to take lots of time, in those ten days leading up to surgery, to do lots of self-care. I even found a surgery meditation and hypnosis CD, called *Stress Free Surgery*.[1] I was willing to try anything, to give myself the best chance of a great outcome and smooth healing. It turned out to be incredibly useful.

1 Thomson, L. (2007) *Stress Free Surgery 2 CD Set: A Self Relaxation Program to Help You Prepare for and Recover from Surgery*. Bancyfelin: Crown House Publishing.

The Arrival of My Penis

Stage One Phalloplasty

The ten days leading up to surgery dragged by. I felt like a kid at Christmas, trying desperately to sleep so that Santa could sneak in and leave presents. Finally, the 23rd August arrived. I had been asked to arrive at the Spire Hospital the evening before my surgery so that they could do all the pre-op checks and get me settled in. This seems rare nowadays and most people just arrive on the morning of their surgery.

Day 1 – Monday

Alex and I decided to set off early as we were driving ourselves mad at home. I was just too nervous and excited to settle. Even though we arrived an hour early, the receptionist showed us straight up to my room. Opening the door, the room was less like a hospital room and more like a hotel. Although surgery here in the UK is funded by our National Health Service, the operation itself takes place in private hospitals – and wow, what a difference that makes! The room was in pristine condition,

light, with a lovely green view and a walk-in shower room. There was a TV and free Wi-Fi, both of which I would come to be incredibly grateful for over the following week.

A few moments after being shown into my room, two nurses, Ada and Gabriella, came to introduce themselves. They were to be my main nurses over the first few days. They were both very warm and friendly and helped to reassure us both, especially Alex, who was ten times as nervous as I was. I would be asleep for the six to eight hours the surgery would take. Poor Alex would just have to pace up and down.

Ada walked us through everything that would happen over my week in the hospital. To give me an idea of how I might feel, she talked about previous patients' experiences. Gabriella gave us a tour of the high-dependency room which I would be transferred to immediately after my surgery. (You are placed in a high-dependency unit and have one-to-one care throughout the first 24 hours as the artery they transplant from the forearm to the phallus needs careful monitoring during this time, to make sure there is adequate blood flow.)

After explaining the procedure and answering our questions, both nurses took my weight, blood pressure, urine, and swabs for MRSA. They also gave me some Hibiscrub® to shower with before going to bed and on waking in the morning. This is to help guard against infection, which is one of the highest causes of failure in lower surgery. I was also given some rather fetching surgery stockings, to guard against thrombosis, and some equally fetching net pants to put on before surgery.

Gabriella told me that Mr Stephens would visit in the morning to have a final talk with me about everything. I would then see the anaesthesiologist and my surgery would begin around 8 am. With that knowledge, I was left to settle in and try to get some sleep. I tossed and turned with a mix of emotions, being

excited for Santa to arrive, but also knowing that Santa was going to punch me in the nuts before giving me my present.

I managed a few hours of restless sleep but was wide awake again by 6 o'clock the following morning, full of nervous energy. I had no doubts about wanting a penis, but by this time I had a ton of doubts about the surgery. There was no denying this was real now; the week ahead would be long and painful, and my gut was on fire with anxiety. I took some deep breaths as I watched the hands of the clock. I focused on the reasons I had chosen this. Thinking about seeing a new penis between my legs made me smile. That smile brought with it a gentle wave of excitement, which tempered the flames of anxiety a little.

Just before 8 o'clock, the first nurse arrived to wish me good morning and to remind me to shower one more time with the Hibiscrub® and then get into my fetching surgery outfit. Before I had time to do that, Mr Stephens arrived. Seeing him in his green gown and blue hair-net was quite a shock, having only ever seen him behind his desk in his office. He ran through what would be happening, as cheerfully as if he were ordering a takeaway.

I was told to expect to be in theatre for around six to eight hours. I was reminded that stage one would involve taking the skin from my left forearm to create the phallus, as well as taking a main artery. A skin graft from underneath my buttocks would then be used as a graft back on the forearm donor site. I would also have one testicle created. I'm one of the rare people to have had a testicle implant at stage one. At the time, the reasoning was that they wanted the testicle to heal properly, ready for the erection device implant at stage three. At stage three they would take away the silicone testicle implant and replace it with the pump device. Back then, doing things in this order was thought to cause fewer complications, but this has since changed and

at the time of writing, here in the UK, no implants are inserted until the final stage (that is, at the same time as the erectile device). Things often change as lower surgery is still a relatively new procedure – trans men going through phalloplasty are still very much pioneers of a rapidly evolving surgery.

Mr Stephens also ran through all the risks of surgery, including the risk of the phallus losing blood flow and dying, the nerves harvested from the arm failing, and losing function of my arm after the graft. He listed these with a smile on his face, reassuring me that these things rarely happened nowadays. I began to wonder if he ever delivered any news without smiling. I signed the consent form and swallowed another hot wave of anxiety. The same questions I had asked myself before my referral resurfaced. Was I sure I needed to do this? Was I sure I couldn't manage to live with and love my vagina, rather than go through this? This one surgery would be just the start of many years of surgery and recovery. Once I started, I couldn't stop. The answer was clearly yes. I needed a penis, whatever the risks, whatever the upheaval. I trusted completely that it was going to be worth it. I pushed myself up off the bed and busied myself with showering and dressing in my surgery gown.

After another agonizing wait, my stomach was now in so many knots I didn't know whether to be sick or fart. Finally, the nurse arrived to tell me it was time. Unlike with top surgery, I was asked to walk to the theatre, instead of being wheeled in my bed. Taking that short walk down the corridor was very peculiar. It felt a little like the 'last march'. However, in some ways, it was also very empowering, as I was actively and consciously walking into the decision to have surgery. I can't deny, though, that the fear was also telling me to run like the wind.

The nurse pushed the doors of the theatre open, revealing a small room with a trolley bed, draped in a blue paper sheet.

I was asked to hop onto the bed and lie down. The intense nature of the first stage was then brought home to me as a cluster of nurses and anaesthetists began attaching numerous wires. First, a nurse attached the regular drip, in the back of my left hand. Next, an arterial line was connected, which would directly take blood pressure readings. Finally, another line was attached to the back of my right hand, so that the post-op morphine dispenser could be wired up later to give me pain relief. The surgical team did their best to reassure me, but by this point I was visibly shaking from a combination of nerves and the fact that the room was heavily air-conditioned and quite chilly. The anaesthetist administered the sleep drug and joked with me, and that is the last thing I remember.

Coming around at what I was told was ten hours later, a tidal wave of pain crashed through my body. Every inch of me was on fire. I was surprised to find that both my arms hurt. I could see my left one, the graft arm, was elevated and inside a giant purple foam sling. I had no idea why my right one was buzzing with pain too. By far the worst pain was in my lower back, which felt like something was sticking into it. I was desperate to move but, of course, I couldn't. The nurses tried to rearrange me, but I was still in agony.

It was explained to me that the reason for everything aching is because you are moved around a lot and put in various positions throughout the surgical process. During the surgery they leave you on your front for a fair while, as they first take the skin grafts from underneath both bum cheeks. Then they turn you onto your back to take the graft from the arm and create the phallus. Other parts of you are bent at strange angles and odd positions – and, boy, did I feel it!

I also realized that I was hurting where I'd had my testosterone injection a few days before surgery. I take Nebido®,

which is notorious for giving you a sore bum. Nebido® is an intramuscular injection, administered into the top of the glutes, and some people find the injection site can ache for a few days. I was usually lucky with my injections and didn't have any pain, but perhaps lying so still and directly on the site for so long had aggravated it. I learned from this experience never to have my injection the week before surgery. Now, for that one mistake, things were made more difficult as I would be stuck on my back for a week with a very sore lower back. This would be made worse by the staples underneath both bum cheeks, where the replacement graft for the arm had been taken from.

My whole body was buzzing with pain and, at that moment, I had that sinking feeling of wondering why on earth I had done this to myself. Thankfully, on account of the nurses moving me a little and giving me more pain relief, the pain eased off to more bearable levels.

Once they had got me more stable, they wheeled me out of the theatre and into the high-dependency unit for the night, where I was more comfortable. I now had a morphine dispenser attached and could use it freely. I was in and out of consciousness, incredibly groggy and not able to focus properly on anything. However, when the nurse checked on me for the first time, I did manage to get an initial glimpse of my pink, swollen, and rather shiny new penis. As my eyes took him in, a warm feeling of joy removed any doubt. I grinned, before passing out again.

Sometime later, I was awoken to what sounded very much like a heartbeat. The noise was like what you hear when a pregnant person has an ultrasound scan. It shocked me wide awake and I realized the sound was coming from my penis. In the early hours after surgery, the main artery, which they take from your arm to give the blood supply to the new penis, must be checked regularly. To make sure the blood supply is working,

the nurse uses a doppler wand, placed on the penis, to listen to the blood pumping through. I knew this would be happening – I had been told that initially it would be every hour. However, I hadn't made the connection with how it would sound, and it did sound exactly like a baby's heartbeat. Reflecting on my conversation with Elizabeth just before surgery, I smiled. Here I had my precious baby penis, changing my life forever.

That first night wasn't as bad as I had imagined it might be. I managed not to have any post-op sickness, for which I was very grateful. I feel rather lucky to generally never have an issue with that. My pain levels weren't too bad. At this early stage, I would describe the pain as uncomfortable and irritating, rather than excruciating. The pain in my back was the most annoying, mostly because I could have avoided it. I was also surprised that my graft arm was barely hurting at all. The only pain in my arm was around my thumb, which felt numb and like the first stage of pins and needles. I asked a nurse about it in the night and she loosened the dressing a bit as it had been cutting in. That helped a great deal.

That first night, I also discovered that the other commonality between birthing a baby and birthing a penis is that you must leave all your dignity at the door. Your penis needs to be checked once an hour with the doppler scanner to make sure the artery is still functioning well and it has a good blood supply.

When the first nurse was settling me in, she said, 'Lovey, I can either wake you every hour and ask your permission, or I can go ahead and do it?'

I laughed and said, 'Just go for it!'

This meant I was free to sleep when I could. Then, during the night, in my drugged-up haze, I would come around to find my penis in a nurse's hand and hear the soft pulse of my beautiful baby penis's heartbeat.

Day 2 – Tuesday

I remained stable and issue-free throughout the night. Therefore, in the morning I was given the go-ahead to be moved from the high-dependency unit back to my regular room. Once there, I was allowed to eat, which was such a relief – I was starving. However, trying to feed yourself when you only have one hand and limited movement is an art. I couldn't push myself up properly with only one arm (the other arm was tied to a pole to elevate it), and when I tried to shuffle up the bed, it pulled like hell on the staples under my bum cheeks. I didn't want to keep ringing the nurses for help, so I learned ways around it. I also learned to choose easier food to eat, after many one-handed failures. Peas, for example, were off the menu for a while. There are only so many times you can chase peas around a plate without wanting to chuck your fork at the wall in frustration.

The pain increased a little as the anaesthesia wore off. However, the grogginess from the anaesthesia, which was quite intense after being under for such a long time, helped me to sleep through most of the pain. Nurses continued to regularly check my penis for its pulse, and I still grinned every time.

A physiotherapy nurse visited and talked me through some bed exercises. The following few days would be long and I wouldn't be able to move much at all. I therefore had a special pressure cuff fitted around my legs, to keep the blood flow going. The physiotherapist showed me some exercises I could do to help keep the blood circulating and to help healing. These were very simple things like pointing my toes and lifting my knees and gently starting to move the fingers on the grafted arm. She also taught me some breathing exercises, reminding me that breathing fully and getting a good supply of oxygen into the body helps with healing. I found this session with the physio

incredibly helpful. It was reassuring to know which bits of me were safe to move, because I had been so scared of hurting anything. Having some exercises to do also helped me to feel more in control and have something productive I could do to help myself and to pass the time. The idea of having four days in bed may sound fantastic, but when you are stuck on your back for that long, it feels like forever and is just so uncomfortable.

By the evening of that first day, the pain was creeping up and I began to ache everywhere from lying in one position. The air mattress and the pressure cuffs didn't seem to be doing much to relieve the pressure and they were also beginning to annoy the hell out of me. That night, I was extremely uncomfortable and had a very bad night. Despite constantly pushing the morphine button, the pain just didn't let up. By the time the following morning arrived, I felt low and fed up.

Day 3 – Wednesday

I called Day 3 'Black Wednesday'. I'd had barely any sleep. Throughout the entire night, I hadn't been able to do more than doze for ten minutes at a time. I'd spent most of the night watching the clock, which seemed to have frozen in time. By now the anaesthesia had worn off, so nothing was numb and nothing was helping me to sleep. I was in so much pain – every inch of me seemed to burn, throb or scream. Being trapped in bed, stuck in the same position, was so uncomfortable I didn't know what to do with myself. With one arm out of use and two heavily stapled arse cheeks, it was impossible to rearrange myself. Besides, if I tried to rearrange myself to be more comfortable, I would end up causing other parts of me to hurt.

Throughout Tuesday night, I'd honestly felt as if I was going

stir-crazy. I'd tried to breathe through it and I'd tried pressing my button for more pain relief. I'd tried distracting myself with my phone. I'd tried meditating. My desperate, bored eyes had found a small dent in the top of the wall opposite the foot of my bed. I'd put all my energy into concentrating on that dot, as a way to get outside my body and to attempt to still my racing mind.

By the time the first light of day began to illuminate the corners of the room, I was miserable. I wished so much that it was Thursday, when I would likely be allowed to move from the bed for the first time. It felt like that day was taking forever to arrive. As I lay there staring at my dot on the wall, I asked myself if having a penis was worth all this. At this point, I could not imagine having any more surgery. This was too much for a human being to bear. I wondered if just the basic phallus would be enough, so I wouldn't have to go through anything else. This was hell. I knew it would be, but knowing and experiencing are two very different things.

The morning turned into the beginning of the working day and the nurses began to do their rounds. At least now I had some distractions and some markers of time rather than just a long, dark night. Breaking the day into units of time felt more manageable. Morning rounds. Breakfast. Penis pulse check. Hot drink delivery. Penis pulse check. Lunch. I had brought some things to do. I had my phone, I had my e-reader, I had music, and most importantly a portable charger so that I didn't need to ask the nurses to charge things. But my concentration was so poor and the pain was too intense for any of my distractions to take my mind off it.

The kind-faced physiotherapist visited again. I confessed how awful I felt, and she said it was often the worst day for people. It helped to know that the way I was feeling was normal. She had a look at my hand on the grafted arm as it was buzzing

with pain. It turned out that the bandage was so tight it was cutting into my thumb. She loosened the bandage and put in some padding. The relief was amazing. The rest of my graft arm didn't hurt much at all. At its worst, my arm just felt like a mild burning, which was uncomfortable but manageable. This may have been because everything else was in so much pain that it paled in comparison. My bloody arse was still the most painful thing in the world. It stung and burned, and the pressure of lying on it was excruciating. Then, there was the issue of my back, which ached so much. I just wanted to get up, walk around and give parts of my body some relief. I couldn't wait for it to be Thursday.

The morning dragged by. Alex couldn't visit that day either, so I had no distraction there. I turned to my phone for comfort, checking into the Facebook trans forums for support and understanding. Having peer support was such an incredible lifeline. Being able to share what I was going through, with people that understood and wouldn't judge me, helped enormously. That afternoon, the smiling face of Mr Stephens arrived at my door.

'How are you doing?' he asked.

'Not too bad,' I lied. I was grateful beyond words to this man, who had just given me a brand-new penis. I wasn't going to be ungrateful and say I felt like crap.

He examined me, commenting that he was very pleased with how everything had gone and the resulting size of my penis. I grinned and told him that I was impressed with the size, too. We had been concerned about the self-harm scars circling my wrist, but they hadn't caused any issues. He reminded me that once the glans was created in stage two, he would be able to work around the scars. Before he said his goodbyes, I told him that I was struggling with the pain and that the morphine button didn't seem to be doing anything. He instructed the nurses to

remove the morphine button and give me Oramorph® instead. This worked so much better for me. I have since learned to just ask when I am in pain rather than trying to be brave. A body heals better when pain is managed, and there is no shame in asking for some relief.

I spent the rest of Wednesday reminding myself, 'This too shall pass.' I felt incredibly grateful to be in recovery and to have some tools from the AA programme to rely on. The one-day-at-a-time approach of the fellowship has got me through many tough periods and was especially helpful through the first few days of stage one. That night, thanks to the change of meds, I managed a few hours of unbroken sleep, which made all the difference.

Day 4 – Thursday

Finally, it was Thursday, that magical day when I would be set free from the irritating chains of the bed. For the first time, I awoke feeling happy. I eagerly awaited the arrival of the morning nurses and breakfast, which I wolfed down. Alex arrived soon after and my heart beamed to see him. I needed a cuddle so much.

Finally, the time came to begin the bed dismount. First, the nurses wanted to change all the dressings on Finn Jr. This would be the first dressing change since surgery, and I was to learn just how complicated it was. For the first six to eight weeks after surgery, your penis must always be at a 45-degree angle. Being at an angle helps to protect the artery and nerves which have been harvested so that the penis gets an adequate blood flow. The penis also cannot hang freely for similar reasons. The sutures, where the penis is attached, must heal before taking any weight. The surgeon fashions a kind of penis cradle with pads

and bandages, to protect the new phallus and support it in this upright position. The nurse began to unravel this willy fortress so that she could clean everything.

'Can you hold your penis for me please, Finn?'

Well, what a wonderful request that was. Nervously and ever so gently, I cupped Finn Jr. in my palm to support him. I stared down at him in absolute awe. This was the first time I had connected with him, other than simply looking at him. To feel his heaviness and his warmth in the palm of my hand made all the doubts melt away. The comparison to holding one's child for the first time was not lost on me here. At that moment, the gratitude and love I experienced for this new part of me made every single bit of pain feel like a drop in the ocean. I continued to stare mesmerized at Finn Jr. whilst the nurse cleaned and replaced the dressings. I was almost scared to breathe in case I moved and injured him in any way. I didn't take my eyes off him until everything had been cleaned and Finn Jr. was safely back in his willy fortress.

Next, the physiotherapist assisted me to slowly swivel my legs to the edge of the bed so that I could sit myself up on the side of the bed. Now let me tell you, this is easier said than done with one arm and a very sore ass. I had barely been able to adjust myself lying back against the pillows, never mind trying to sit up completely. With very slow movements and the grace of a baby elephant, I finally managed to get my legs off the side of the bed and sit upright. The pain in my arse cheeks stung like hell and I was exhausted already.

After a moment catching my breath and making sure I wasn't going to pass out, I finally managed to get on my feet. With the physiotherapist on one side and Alex on the other, I took a few tentative steps. I stood for all of three minutes and walked barely two feet, but it felt amazing. To take the pressure off my back

and my stapled bum cheeks was heaven. Getting back into bed proved to be equally challenging. I felt like I had run an entire marathon and I slept for a straight hour after that.

I got up again later and sat in the chair for dinner, but it was too painful on my stapled bum to stay in that position for long so I got back into bed pretty soon afterwards. Lying on my back was easier as it took the pressure off the bum staples. Just having the choice, though, to get up and lie back down, was so much help. At least now I had some freedom returned.

Mr Stephens visited again later in the day to check that Finn Jr. was a good colour and that the pulse was still strong. He reported he was pleased with how everything was healing and that it looked good.

Whenever I had privacy, I would lift the covers and gaze at my new penis. It felt both surreal and ordinary all at once. It looked like it had always been there, but at the same time it didn't feel quite like it belonged to me yet.

Day 5 – Friday

Friday was the best day. The darkness of Wednesday had faded, and Thursday had filled me with new optimism. I was still in extreme discomfort, but by comparison with before, and especially with a stronger mind, the pain was more manageable. I think the relief of getting out of bed helped and the tiredness from it meant I slept soundly.

That morning the nurse removed the catheter, which was such a relief. It had been giving me a ton of pain and making me feel like I need the toilet constantly. I would discover over my next surgeries that my body just does not get on well with catheters.

As well as a catheter, I also had a drain (called a Penrose drain) attached to the shaft of my penis. This was to help get any blood out of the phallus. This drain was also removed. Additionally, the cannula was removed from my hand. This just left the stent, which was also in the shaft of the penis and would come out before I left on Sunday. It felt good to be getting unhooked from things – like I was being set free.

However, the pain now was becoming more intense. The worst bit at this point was between my legs in the newly created testicle. I think the fact that I was moving, as lovely as that was, was also causing things to pull and hurt. The staples in my bum were absolute agony, especially when getting up off the bed and then back onto it. My arm didn't hurt an awful lot unless it was lowered, and then it would begin to throb. On the whole, when elevated, it remained more like a background slight burning with occasional sharp pain.

My fingers were mildly swollen. I could move them and was told to exercise them by touching the thumb tip to each finger. At this point, I had a lot of pins and needles in my hand. I had normal sensation in my fingers but no sensation in my thumb, which continued to be numb. On expressing concern about this, I was reassured that numbness was often common in the early days.

As amazing as it was to be free from the catheter, I now had to negotiate the toilet. Going for a pee was such hard work and incredibly complicated. Let me tell you that sitting on the loo is a logistical nightmare. Having a stapled bum, a willy fortress and only one arm turns a toileting outing into a major sporting event. Before surgery, I had worried that I might need someone else to wipe my arse. I was relieved to find out I could do this myself. Saying that, though, it wasn't easy. I found putting the toilet roll in my sling meant easier access to it. That was one

issue sorted out; the other issue was trying not to pee on my staples and cause even more stinging.

I could see my progress now, though, especially with my walking, which was much easier than it had been the day before. This little bit of independence – managing to walk to the toilet alone and wipe my own bum – was a gift from heaven.

The doubt I had felt on that awful Black Wednesday was now a distant memory. I've learned that doubt is part of every stage when you are low and in pain. By Friday, although worn out, I had reached a place of acceptance of the pain levels and my level of incapacitation. I'd learned how best to manage the pain and found myself more able to sit back and grin about the fact that I now had a penis.

Alex visited later that day and we spoke a bit about how he felt about my penis. He said he was pleasantly surprised to find how much he liked the look of it, even in its current battered shape. It was a relief to hear that, but of course only time would tell.

Day 6 – Saturday

Saturday was my sixth and penultimate day in the hospital. I woke up feeling hot and achy and my bum wounds were stinging. By this point, I was familiar with waking up feeling awful and I had learnt that it passed. The initial morning awakening and the first hour are often rough, but then things improve as adrenaline and meds kick in.

The main event on Saturday was to have a shower. This was my first shower since Monday, when I was admitted. I was looking forward to this. Soon after breakfast, there was a knock at my door.

'Mornin', Finn. Are ye ready for yer shower?'

Before I got a chance to answer, the nurse was bustling around the room, moving furniture, pulling off sheets, grabbing clothing, whilst talking at me monologue-style with a thick Scottish accent.

I was up and out of that bed so fast and bustled across the corridor to a large, walk-in disabled shower. Once naked, all I could do was hold Finn Jr. with one hand to support him and hold my graft arm in the air to avoid it getting wet. I was quite literally at the mercy of this enthusiastic nurse as I had no hands spare. I didn't have any concerns or embarrassment about her doing this because I was concentrating so hard on holding on tight (but not too tight) to Finn Jr. Apart from the brief hold of my penis when the dressings were changed on Tuesday, this was the first time I'd properly held my penis and seen him without any bandage. He felt so heavy and a bit squishy. He looked so delicate and I was terrified of letting go and him falling off.

The nurse and I negotiated the washing and drying process quite well, until the final phase of returning me to my room, when we had this rather comedic moment of me holding the towel around my waist, with her hand through the gap in the front of the towel holding my penis whilst we crossed the corridor back to my room. I could still only shuffle, but my feet moved like lightning for fear she would pull my penis off if I didn't catch up. I was both relieved to be clean and glad that it was over.

After the shower, everything was redressed. I managed to get a pair of loose gym shorts on for the first time. This gave me a lot to smile about as it was so wonderful to look down and see a bulge in my pants. I spent the rest of that day constantly staring and smiling at it. I couldn't believe I had my own natural bulge.

Later, Mr Stephens came in for a final look at everything.

He also gave me a rundown of what I would need to do at home after my discharge from hospital. He reminded me to keep Finn Jr. elevated for the first six weeks until I had my post-op consultation. He told me that I would need the staples in my bum removed after ten days, at my local health clinic. He also reminded me to do my arm exercises, to gradually straighten my arm and get the use of my hand back. I knew it was going to be a long recovery time, but at that moment, having it all spelled out like this, it felt like an eternity.

That afternoon, I had the the first arm-dressing change. This was the bit I was dreading the most: seeing the graft for the first time. I had seen lots of pictures of other people's arms immediately post-op, so I knew it was going to look pretty terrifying. I was afraid I might be sick or break down in tears, so I braced myself. The nurse began unravelling the bandage, which went on for what felt like ages before she finally reached the special blue gauze protecting the new skin. I took a deep breath as she removed the final piece of dressing and revealed a very raw and pink-looking arm. However, seeing it was not as bad as I had expected. I think it's different when it's your own arm. It looked like a good, clean, neat and healthy graft. I knew it would look worse as healing progressed because it scabs over as it heals and can go rather black. However, after seeing it for the first time and not feeling as shocked as I had feared I might, I felt more confident I could deal with it.

I did get a little emotional after it was redressed. Some of the hardest parts of transition are the compromises we must make to be whole and happy. Now that I care so much about myself, compared with the old days when I would abuse my body with drink, drugs and self-harm, I feel bad for inflicting such a serious injury to my body. However, I'm aware that it's an unavoidable part of the transition process and, my word, it's worth it. I do

feel that it is necessary, though, to accept, grieve, and thank my body for its sacrifice. I would never have the same arm I had pre-surgery and I would need to mourn that loss.

Day 7 – Sunday

Finally, Sunday, my seventh and final day in hospital, arrived. As long as everything was assessed to be okay, I would be discharged. The day began with a parade of various nurses and doctors. First to arrive was Lisa, the same kind physiotherapist as before. She wanted to check my walking and make sure that I was able to manage the stairs. We waddled off together, down the corridor and into the hallway where the stairs to the lower floor began. Slowly, we took one step at a time and completed one group of steps down. Then, even more slowly, we climbed up the stairs again. The staples on my bum made lifting each leg very difficult and painful. Also, only being able to use one arm meant I was less balanced. We practised a few stairs up and down; then, when Lisa was happy with my endeavours, we slowly waddled back to my room. I sat in the chair and promptly fell asleep.

About half an hour later, Gabriella knocked on my door and came in. I sleepily smiled and said hello. I would be sad to say goodbye to her as she had been so kind and understanding throughout my whole stay. She gave me all the medications I would need and also a letter for my doctor. As soon as I got home, my local GP and nurses would be looking after my wounds. I would have to make sure that they followed the instructions exactly. I felt nervous about this prospect. I expected that with the rarity of my surgery, nurses might well struggle to know how to best treat me. I was as prepared as possible to tackle that one.

Gabriella also gave me tons of spare dressings and a strong painkiller for the way home. Sid, Alex's dad, had kindly offered to pick me up and drive me back to Oxford. It was about an hour's journey and I anticipated it might be a little uncomfortable.

I had been given lots of advice from friends who'd had phallo on the best way to manage the drive, so I had a plan. When Sid and Alex arrived, we reclined the front seat and put lots of padding everywhere. It worked well, and the drive home went smoothly enough. The hardest part – the surgery and getting well enough for discharge – was over.

Adjusting at Home and the Early Recovery Phase

Arriving home, I was exhausted but relieved to be back in my flat with Alex and to have my home comforts. However, as uncomfortable as the hospital had been, at least it was designed for recovery, whereas my home, of course, wasn't. At the hospital, I'd got used to the best ways to sit and move, the hospital bed was electric, and there were places to hang my arm. At home in my flat, there was none of that.

I had to rediscover new comfortable places to sit and new ways to get in and out of bed and on and off the sofa. Oh, boy, that sofa – how I hated it! When you have staples in both bum cheeks, a throbbing testicle, and only one arm, there is no easy or graceful way to get up off a sofa. I looked like a beached whale, flailing my one good arm and slowly wriggling from side to side until I could stand. Luckily, I had a sense of humour – you really do need to have one to survive lower surgery.

The other thing I wasn't prepared for was the responsibility of caring for Finn Jr. I mean, I knew all the instructions – that bit was okay – but I wasn't prepared for all the worrying I would do. And there was much to worry about. Was he at the right

angle? Were the bandages too tight? Was I handling him right? Was I causing him any damage when he was wrapped in my sexy net pants?

The analogy of having a new baby is one that really does apply to having a new penis. It comes with only the most basic of manuals, and suddenly being responsible for caring for it (making sure it's warm but not restricted, at a 45-degree angle, clean, etc.) does feel overwhelming.

Alex and I had our first attempt at Finn Jr.'s night care the first evening I arrived home. Getting ready for bed, we were both so nervous. First, we gently cleaned Finn Jr. and then made sure he was nicely padded and at a 45-degree angle. Then there was the issue of where to hang my donor arm, which also needed to be elevated to prevent swelling. I wished we had thought about this sooner – I really recommend sorting this out in advance. We tried various options: hanging my arm on a chair, using a floor lamp, using the clothes airer. None of these worked, and Alex and I were both giggling with exhaustion. Finally, we moved a bookcase next to my side of the bed and attached a hook and some string. This worked perfectly. Now I just had to get some sleep, which also proved to be challenging.

That first night I needed to struggle out of bed to pee every hour. I've come to accept this as a normal post-surgery reaction for me. The constant peeing is likely because my body is trying to flush out the toxins from all the medications. It is also likely because I swell a great deal after surgery. Eventually, the water that my body was holding onto had to come back out. Whatever the reason, it was bloody frustrating. Trying to get out of a regular bed, which couldn't be raised and lowered like a hospital bed, was incredibly difficult and excruciatingly painful. Also, the constant weeing was making my bum dressings damp and causing them to lift. Not to mention the piercing, stinging pain

that moving and dampness caused on my bum wounds. I woke up on that first morning home feeling pretty fed up.

It had been a few days since I'd had my last shower with the over-enthusiastic Scottish nurse. So, Alex and I decided it would be a good idea to attempt my first home shower, especially because of how much the dressings over my bum staples were lifting. Besides, we thought it might be nice and soothing for me. After all, who doesn't feel better after a shower? How wrong I was.

There are people who somehow manage to recover from surgery alone. I have absolutely no idea how they do it and I certainly do not recommend it. If you have a friend you trust, ask them, bribe them, because nobody should struggle through this by themselves. It's just all too complicated. I only had one usable hand, which I could work around most things, but once undressed, that one hand had to hold Finn Jr. as he was not allowed to hang free for the first three weeks. The grafts taken from underneath each bum cheek made bending impossible, and I couldn't lift my legs or use my arms. Seriously, without Alex I have no idea how I would have coped with the enormity of stage one. No matter what happened with us later in our relationship, nothing ever takes away the immense gratitude I have for him for helping me through the toughest few months of this surgery.

The first shower was a complete comedy sketch. Our shower was an over-the-bath one. This meant that I had to lift a leg over into the bath, followed by the other one – a seemingly simple task, unless you have two tightly stapled arse cheeks, one out-of-action arm and a new penis in a willy fortress. After first getting naked, I now stood with my good hand supporting Finn Jr. and – with the sling removed for the shower – holding my graft arm against my chest. With both hands busy, I then somehow had to negotiate getting into this bloody bath whilst

holding onto Jr. for dear life. Alex held onto me as best he could, but I was just too wobbly standing on one leg. Instead, we tried with Alex holding onto Finn Jr., thereby giving me a free hand to hold the wall and support myself getting in. This worked better. Once both legs were in the bath, Alex handed Finn Jr. back to me. During the washing process there was lots of passing Finn Jr. back and forth in order to be able to reach different areas and turn around. This caused much hilarity, but it was also exhausting. We soon realized that showering every day would not be possible. Instead, I showered on alternate days, using baby wipes to wash on the days in-between.

It wasn't just the showering that was arduous work. Redressing everything was a painful marathon too. The bum grafts were hell on earth. They stung like salt pressed into a fresh graze. The hospital had told us to shower and then pat dry the dressings, but the trouble is, when you pee, you can't help but get them wet; and once they've peeled away from the skin, they stop being hygienic and need to be changed. Being a hairy guy, taking off two dressings, each of which is 12 centimetres in length, is excruciating, let alone the fact that it also pulls the staples. I later discovered something called Zoff®, which is a little wipe which removes adhesive. Using these to help remove dressings from a hairy butt makes it much easier.

Dressings are another thing that you need to think outside the box about. The dressings they give you are expensive and specialized; a lot of GPs won't prescribe them without an express request. I recommend before any surgery that you meet with your doctor and make them aware that there will be lots of requests for different meds and dressings. If they put it on your file, it makes it so much easier when you ring up and say, 'My consultant has asked me to get a prescription for x dressing, and I have a note on my file to allow these requests.' This just takes

the hassle out of asking for things from your GP. There are lots of similar dressings to those you are given which are less costly, so that's an option too. I recommend that as soon as you are home from hospital you get spares. It's enough of a hassle taking care of yourself, let alone trying to get to the GP for dressings.

Having enough dressings means that if they are loose, as they were with me after a couple of days, once out of the shower you can ask a willing friend to change them. If you have to do this on your own, I suggest contacting your doctor to see if a district nurse can come out every couple of days to correspond with your shower days.

With all the stinging and pee on the dressings, I was quite concerned about how the wounds would look. However, on our first change of them (I say 'our' but it was poor Alex who had to delicately peel the little terrors off me), I was very pleasantly surprised to find that the wound was clean and healthy-looking, and very neat too.

After that first home shower, I felt so much better. I even managed to get comfortable sat on the sofa – the bum pain was also much better. I think I just needed to adapt to the home environment and to feel confident in looking after myself. Alex and I both felt quite vulnerable and scared to be looking after so many different sore areas on me. The shower experience, no matter how comical, had boosted our confidence and belief in our ability to manage the delicate early weeks.

Over the next few days, we settled into our rhythm of showering every other day and baby wiping in the days in-between. The pain gradually became more manageable as I got into a routine with pain relief medication at home and found comfortable ways to sit. Sleeping remained an issue – with so many areas affected, it's hard to find a comfortable position, and I'm not the best at sleeping on my back.

Most of my pain in the early days was concentrated underneath my penis. Where I had the testicular implant, everything had swollen. My T-dick had got squashed in-between all the swelling and that was sensitive too.

My graft arm was very achy and incredibly swollen. I was told to expect this; in fact, it can take a year for the arm to normalize. I just elevated it whenever I was sat resting, and that made the swelling go down a bit.

After a couple of days at home, at ten days post-op, I noticed some oozing at the base of my phallus. It was a bit smelly too. Mr Stephens had told me to email St Peter's if there were any issues and to include pictures. With Alex's help, I took some pictures with my phone and then emailed them across. A couple of hours later, Mr Stephens replied. He advised that I shouldn't worry too much; the phallus looked healthy and it's better if it oozes than if the fluid stays inside. He recommended starting a course of Augmentin® antibiotic and using a dressing at the base called Kaltostat® to soak up the fluid. I rang my GP surgery and arranged a telephone call. As I had set everything up prior to surgery, getting the medication and dressings was straightforward.

Alex and I decided to rearrange the willy fortress, moving the padding a bit to allow air to circulate better. Everything was so hot down there and all that bulky padding likely wasn't helping the area to dry out. Working out the right amount of padding and what underwear to use requires a lot of trial and error. The net pants they use in hospital are not at all comfortable. I had to be careful about the end of the phallus not getting squashed, especially as I couldn't yet feel my penis to tell if it hurt. I initially tried boxer shorts, but I found that as the leg openings were loose, the dressings and Finn Jr. wouldn't stay put. I found boxer trunks to be much better. The legs on boxer trunks are snugger, so everything stayed in place better. I made sure to choose a

slightly bigger size of trunks, though, because I needed them to support, but also not to be too tight.

I have to say that, of all the things I had prepared for, I had not prepared enough for just how much I would worry. I often found myself getting freaked out and overwhelmed, worrying about whether I was doing things right. Was I elevating the phallus in the correct way? Was I using enough padding? Was I elevating the arm enough? There was just so much to look after, and I wanted to do all I could to avoid any infections or complications.

The first two weeks were exhausting, frustrating and painful. However, at 12 days post-op I turned a rather large corner. Having begun to get more sleep at night and managing to be a little more mobile, I felt so much better in myself. It's important to move around, but of course it's also incredibly challenging. I ventured outside for the first time – just to the end of the path and back, but it felt like a huge achievement.

However, this journey is one of peaks and troughs, and reaching two weeks post-op I sank into a deep low mood. The infection at the base of my phallus began to really get to me. It smelled a lot and everything was stinging. I just wanted to bawl my eyes out. I was still taking the antibiotics and using the dressings that Mr Stephens had suggested. Logically, I knew it would pass but I was just sick of it. My resolve was shaky and my mood was suffering. I know that this was all due to fear. I was terrified of something going dreadfully wrong and losing my penis. I knew that was rare but, still, I could be one of the rare ones. I just wanted everything to be okay. Everything between my legs looked like an angry mess and I was sad, scared and frustrated. Alex was incredible during all of this, reassuring me and spending ages cleaning around the infected area. It was far too complicated for me to reach.

Two weeks post-op – staple removal

At two weeks post-op, I was due to have the staples taken out of my bum. This was something I was both dreading and looking forward to. Dreading, because I expected it might be painful, and looking forward because I was sick of the bum pain. I had booked a double appointment with the nurse because I was also going to have my arm redressed for the first time since leaving hospital.

Getting to the doctor's surgery was quite a mission. Neither Alex nor I drove at the time. My GP surgery was about a 20-minute walk away, but there was no way I could walk that. We had decided beforehand to hire a wheelchair so that Alex could push me to appointments. Well, I hadn't considered that just sitting and being pushed would be painful enough in itself.

I had bought a thick memory foam and gel cushion for sitting on the sofa and we used that on the wheelchair. I carefully lowered myself into it and managed to get into a position where I could sit without too much pain. Once I was settled, we set off, very slowly.

Alex did his best, bless him, but I felt every tiny bump and rough area on those Oxfordshire pavements. Then, of course, there was getting up and down kerbs. Luckily, we found it all highly amusing and managed to laugh through the difficulty and discomfort. By the time we both arrived at my GP surgery, we were both worn out. However, the worst was not over.

'Finlay Games?'

The nurse first went through my notes with me, making sure she knew what was to be done. Then, with a lot of effort, I managed to get myself up onto the trolley bed and half onto my side, so that the staple extraction could begin.

I had spoken with many trans guys about the staple removal.

The most common comment was that it was uncomfortable but okay. Well, I must have been a special case because, my word, it hurt like hell getting those little demons out of my arse. They weren't just under my cheeks either; they went from the side of my hips and around into my groin. The staples going into my groin were the absolute worst. I just bit down and clenched my fists. The nurse was so kind and so apologetic. I told her it was okay, just do it. What else could either of us do but brave it and keep at it. At 30 minutes in, we weren't even halfway done on the staples and we had my arm to redress. The nurse kindly moved all her appointments to another nurse, so she was free to work on me.

Once the final staples were out, all three of us breathed a sigh of relief. In total, it took just over 45 minutes to get those staples out (there were 99 of them). Many of them had been overgrown by my skin, which is what caused much of the problem. I am a super-fast healer, so it might have been better for me if I had asked someone to have a look at the staples earlier, to see if I might benefit from having them out sooner.

The nurse gave the stapled areas a good look over and said that they looked great. She examined all my other wounds too. There were some weepy areas, especially across the top of my pubic bone where the skin was tight and the wound wasn't holding closed. However, the nurse said they should be fine, especially because I was still on the antibiotics. Alex took some pictures for my records and to keep an eye on the healing progress. The nurse at the hospital had advised us to do that. That way, we could easily see improvement from one day to the next and spot any troublesome areas.

It felt reassuring to have someone with medical knowledge say that the weeping, in my bum wounds and under the base of my phallus, was normal, looked okay and would be fine. Finally,

the nurse put iodine strips across the entire length of my bum wounds for extra antibiotic protection and then placed fresh dressings on them.

The relief at having the staples gone made the pain worthwhile. Climbing off the trolley and sitting back in the chair next to the nurse was so much easier without the staples pulling. Now we just had the arm to tackle. The arm was more new territory for the nurse. It isn't commonplace to deal with phalloplasty surgery – most nurses will never have come across it. For this reason, it is really sensible to make sure you are as knowledgeable as possible so that you can guide the people caring for you through exactly what needs to be done.

The nurse prepared an area on her desk ready to tackle the arm. I swivelled to my left side, took my arm out of the sling and placed it gently onto the plastic hygiene sheet she had laid on her desk. As the nurse began to unroll the bandage on my arm, I felt the same nervousness as I had the first time it was undressed in hospital. Of course, I wanted the best outcome possible for my graft. I had seen many guys whose graft hadn't taken properly and had left raised and purple scarring. I knew that was my worst-case scenario and I had prepared for it as best as I could, but I would rather be one of the lucky ones who healed well.

Finally, the bandage was off, and just the final layer, a moist gauze bandage designed for burns, remained. The nurse gently peeled it off. The arm looked purple and not at all like my own, but I was surprised at how, in just a week, it was beginning to improve. Areas were beginning to go black and scab, which is normal and supposed to happen. All in all, it looked good. The nurse followed the instructions carefully and just cleaned the arm up a bit and redressed it.

After having the staples out and the arm freshly redressed, I felt like a new man. My mood, which had been so low, felt like

it had been lifted at last. Alex and I made our way home, which was much easier when sitting in the wheelchair without a bum full of metal staples.

However, the next morning on redressing everything after my shower, we found that the incision line on my pubic area had come open. The practice nurse we saw did say this could happen as it was angry and gaping when she took the staples out. I didn't know whether it would need stitches, so I rang the doctor's surgery and they kindly booked me an appointment for 2 pm.

This time, Alex and I got a lift to the doctor's. I was still worn out from the day before, and neither of us could face using the wheelchair. This time, we saw a different nurse, but she was just as kind and patient as the first one. She tried her best to close the area with Steri-Strips™, but as the area there is quite taut, it wouldn't stay closed. The nurse felt that stiches wouldn't be needed, so instead she packed the area and said that it would heal from underneath. Unfortunately, it would likely leave a bigger scar area, but, hopefully, as it was on my pubic area, once the hair regrew it would be hidden.

Three weeks post-op

Once the staples were out, the week that followed was much easier to deal with. I was able to get up and down off the bed and sofa much more easily. And I was more mobile in general. My giant swollen testicle was now all that was holding me back from walking like a human rather than a penguin.

Being able to move more easily meant that at last I could begin to increase my time outside. I needed to escape the four walls and have a change of scenery. Having the wheelchair made this so much easier. Alex and I would head to the local shops for

a coffee. I could waddle for as long as I could manage it and then, when it became too much, I could sit in the wheelchair again. This meant I could gradually increase the amount I walked. Hiring that wheelchair was one of the best decisions we had made.

When it came to the third redressing of my arm, which was done weekly at this stage, I even made it all the way to the doctor's without needing the chair. Granted, I looked as though I had soiled myself walking, but, hey, it's progress, not perfection.

I was less worried on this third change of the arm dressing. It still looked battered and it was hard to imagine it ever looking normal again, but it was healing well. After the redressing, I emailed Mr Stephens as requested and received a reassuring reply that it was looking fine and that the healing appeared to be on schedule.

My main worry at this stage was the movement and use of my arm. I was still routinely doing the exercises they had prescribed before I left hospital. This was to touch my thumb to each finger and wiggle my fingers. Also, I was to gently straighten the arm, but it still would not straighten completely. I wasn't allowed to rotate the arm or the wrist yet, due to the risk to the graft. The wrist was the most painful area of the arm – when I wiggled my fingers, I got a sharp pain in my wrist. My thumb and the area around it were still mostly numb too. I was told that all these things were normal, but it's hard not to be worried that normal function will never return. I was looking forward to my post-op appointment to discuss these concerns and to be told what else I could do to heal and strengthen my hand.

In general, at three weeks, everything now seemed to be healing well. My staple-free bum was still a joy. The incision had stayed closed and was drying up nicely. The bruising had really come out, though. It was still sore to sit on, but not as bad as it had been with the staples in.

The area on my pubic bone, above my phallus, that came open was also healing well. Under the instructions of Mr Stephens, we were still dressing it daily with Kaltostat®. This was drying it out and you could see that it was healing from underneath.

There were still plenty of other oozy, smelly areas, under the phallus and around the hole where I had the stent. However, by this point I had just got used to them and they had stopped worrying me as much. All of these areas did show signs of drying out, though, and seeing that progress was a relief.

My new penis was looking amazing. The swelling was going down, meaning he was softer and looked more like a penis than a fat, overly cooked sausage. I noticed, perhaps because of the way he was stitched, that he was bending more on the left side. I kept having to straighten him in his willy fortress as he still needed to be kept at a 45-degree angle to protect the nerve. I felt myself beginning to bond with this new, pink, shiny baby. He was feeling more like mine and more securely attached.

All in all, Week 3 saw a big improvement in everything. I was sleeping better, moving better, and feeling far more resilient against the trials of early post-op recovery. I dared to think that the worst might be over.

Four weeks post-op

Reaching four weeks post-op, it was time at last to have my post-op check-up in London. This was the farthest I had travelled so far, and I was quite nervous. I decided to get the coach rather than the train, just to make it a little easier.

Arriving at St Peter's, I saw Julie, who pretty much did the same thing that my practice nurse had been doing, redressing the arm and the dressings around the phallus. However, it was

good to have reassurance that everything was healing well and on track. It was also useful to ask questions, to have some concerns laid to rest, and some next steps made clear.

I shared my concerns about the bend in the middle of Finn Jr. Julie reassured me that it was probably swelling. She said that once the swelling reduced and gravity pulled my penis straight, the bend would likely sort itself out. Julie also added that even if the bend remained, it could be fixed later. Having the erectile prosthesis at the final stage would also pull my penis straight if there was a bend.

Julie also had a good look at all the oozy areas and reassured me. She said that they were minor and that it's all part of healing as the wounds close and the stitches dissolve. The hole that opened above my phallus had healed quickly and was now just a shallow scab. As Finn Jr. was still quite swollen, Julie advised me not to let him hang freely just yet, but to give it a couple more weeks.

Julie redressed my arm too, and it looked good. It was starting to dry out even more and I could see the beginnings of fresh pink skin through a few gaps in the scabbing. Julie advised me to keep the arm in the sling and elevated until the arm and graft looked more normal. The arm would need weekly dressing for a few more weeks.

I also asked about arm movement and exercise and was again reassured that I was on track. Julie told me that it can take a while until it's possible to straighten the arm, and also that numbness and pain are to be expected for some time. She advised me to continue doing what I had already been doing: touching my thumb to each finger and straightening the arm as much as possible. Julie also reasserted that I was not to rotate the wrist yet.

Finally, she had a look at my buttock incisions. They were

tight and bruised but healing very well. I asked about using a moisturizer on them to ease the tightness, but I was informed that I shouldn't moisturize anywhere just yet. I also asked about bathing as some guys seemed to be told that salt baths are helpful. Julie said that it was still too early for me to do that. I couldn't wait to have a soak in the bath and smell like a normal human being again.

I had expected this appointment to include having a catheter tube passed down the middle of my phallus to clear the urethral tube, and then to be taught to do this myself at home. Other guys, whose surgery I was following, had this happen. Flushing is an important part in keeping the tube open and clean until the hook-up of the urethral tube in stage two. Julie was not set to do this today, but said that she would ask Mr Stephens and that I should receive another appointment soon to sort that out, which I did.

All in all, it was an incredibly positive appointment. I felt very reassured to know that everything was on track. I also felt more confident in the knowledge that I was doing all the right things and knowing what to continue doing over the next few weeks.

Five weeks post-op

The following week, on Julie's advice, I gradually began to reduce the support under Finn Jr. In doing this, the bend and crease in the left side of him straightened out a lot. The stitches were still pulling a little bit around the base, but only bleeding a tiny bit. For the first time, I began to trust that my penis wouldn't fall off. I noticed a big decrease in swelling this week. I do tend to swell a lot, but at last my penis was starting to look less

swollen, especially around the base. I would soon be able to let Finn Jr. hang free.

Having the swelling go down meant walking also improved. Also, with the bum incision line getting less sore, sitting was now far less of a problem. One tiny area on the incision line remained open and sore but it was improving daily. At five weeks, all of this meant that, finally, my mobility was far easier.

I had the arm redressed by my practice nurse again and it was surprising to see the progress in just a week since Julie had redressed it. The scabbing was dry and cracks had begun to reveal lots of healthy pink skin, which was amazing to see. I emailed pictures to Mr Stephens as usual and received a reply to say how pleased he was with how it looked too. I also asked him about the flushing of the phallus. It was frustrating that I hadn't had my flushing done earlier as I really didn't want to go all the way back to London. However, Mr Stephens said he would post a flushing kit out to me as it's easy to do. I was a bit worried about doing it myself, but agreed anyway. Later that day, however, the phone rang, and it was Julie. She was ringing to arrange an appointment to get me flushed through. Talk about the left hand not knowing what the right hand is doing! Anyway, I agreed to travel to London as I'd prefer they did it rather than me in case of any problems, plus it would give me a chance to ask some more questions about recovery.

One of the main problems in going through phalloplasty at the time was the lack of information as to what should be happening and when. It was often a cause of anxiety for me not to know exactly when to stop elevating the arm, when to let Finn Jr. hang free, when to flush, etc. It would have been very useful to have had clear guidelines around these key issues. Of course, everyone heals at different rates, so things will happen at slightly different times, but a general guide would have alleviated a lot

of stress and guesswork. Clear guidelines would also be useful to pass on to the local care team, as so often they have no idea how best to support trans people post-surgery.

It is important to remember that phallo is still a relatively young and rapidly progressing surgery. There are also an increasing number of trans people opting for lower surgery. These combined factors mean that the London team is under enormous pressure, as it is the only clinic offering surgery. Many of these issues are being addressed as the surgery and the team evolve.

My advice to anyone is that with this surgery you need to be very proactive. You need to do your research and you need to not be afraid of asking questions and chasing things up. This is so important to keep yourself healthy and on track. I have to say that I am impressed with Mr Stephens – he always answered my emails quickly, so that's one saving grace; that and our fabulous Facebook surgery forums.

Six weeks post-op

I found myself in another mood dip at six weeks post-op. First stage phalloplasty recovery just seems to drag on forever and ever. Coping with the still restricted movement and the use of only one arm is exhausting. I also think that I am someone who has a reaction to anaesthesia in terms of it lowering my mood. At six weeks, I hit a slump where, although I could see improvements, there was still so far to go that it seemed life might never be normal again.

I was trying my best to return to my daily routine, including to attempt to return to my studies. Thank goodness I am an Open University student. Distance-learning at least meant I could be flexible about when and where I studied. I just kept

taking things one day at a time and doing what I could daily, whilst reminding myself that I was getting better and would continue to do so.

The one area where I could see the most astounding recovery was my arm. It was incredible to see its progress each week. When I had my redressing at six weeks, most of the scabs were lifting off, with lots of gorgeous pink, shiny skin underneath. I felt so amazed at my body's ability to heal like this, and so incredibly grateful.

I returned to London to have the flushing done. I saw a different nurse, Katie, this time. I felt very nervous about this appointment. I was worried that the cavity through my penis, created ready for the urethral hook-up, might have healed closed. Katie took a catheter tube and inserted it down the head of my penis and out through the new opening which came out by my T-dick. It needed some wiggling, but it went through okay. It wasn't painful – there was just an odd feeling as she pushed it through, and I felt it pop when it cleared through the other end. Honestly, it wasn't painful, just very strange.

Katie then gave me a syringe and instructed me to take some warm water and just flush it through from the head of my penis and to do this daily. I was to continue to do this until I had the urethral hook-up at stage two, just to keep everything clean and clear.

Katie was wonderful and answered all the questions, especially the ones I had about my arm. She said I could now rotate the wrist gently and gradually increase all movement of the arm. I could also ditch the sling for much of the time and allow the arm to be used normally. However, she advised perhaps still wearing it for a while outside the house, just to get protection from knocks until the graft had fully healed. Katie also encouraged me to keep elevating the arm when sat at home to reduce

the swelling in the hand. My arm and hand were swelling a lot – at times, my hand was almost ball-shaped. The most exciting thing was to be told I could now soak both myself and my arm in a salt bath. I was advised to first soak my arm separately, in a bowl of warm water. This would encourage the scabs to come off and promote healing. I very much looked forward to doing that. In terms of redressing it, Katie suggested having one more visit with my own practice nurse, and then, as long as there were no open wounds, I could leave the arm undressed and just use a loose bandage to protect it.

I returned home from London and the first thing I did was soak my arm in a bowl of water. As I did, lots of old, dead skin lifted off, which was disgusting and satisfying in equal measure. It was wonderful to see glorious new, pink skin revealed and my arm looked markedly improved.

Next, I ran a shallow bath, filled it with some salts, and sat blissfully in it for ten minutes. It was absolute heaven and for the first time, I felt properly clean and smelt fresh. Afterwards, as Katie instructed, I was also okay to use moisturizer. I used the same product that I used for my top surgery: tamanu oil. It really is such a lovely oil and it felt so soothing on my tight bum incisions. This picked up my mood no end. To feel clean and soothed was such a simple but enormous pleasure.

Seven weeks post-op

Week 7 saw a dramatic shift in mood. Being able to flush through my penis and have a short soak in a bath meant that the awful smell from the oozy areas was so much better.

The only area that was still oozing slightly was down the side of my ball in my groin area. There was no visible wound,

but when I wiped there, a bit of blood appeared. It was likely just where the sutures in my groin area were still healing. The trouble is, there are some areas of the body that are prone to staying wet because of where they are, and therefore take longer to heal. The only thing you can really do about this is to spend as much time as possible naked, with your legs spread, if your living arrangements will allow it. Poor Alex came home to some right states some days, I can tell you.

The good thing is that at this point everything moved from feeling painful to just feeling sore. This also dramatically improved my walking, from waddling penguin to cowboy horse rider.

Finn Jr. was still swollen at this point but nowhere near as much as he had been. By Week 7, he was much softer and moveable but still very heavy. I began to walk around letting him hang free, but I was still grabbing him on occasion, for fear of him falling off.

Noting sensation at this point, I was surprised to find that all my original areas had the same sensation. However, there was no sensation on my penis as yet, but that was to be expected.

All my other incisions seemed to turn a massive corner at seven weeks too. My tummy and groin incisions were completely healed and the areas around them were completely numb. My bum incisions were looking remarkable too, and massaging them was helping it all feel less tight. At this point, I began moisturizing and massaging all the healed incisions. I also started using Kelo-Cote®, a silicone-based scar treatment gel. I used Kelo-Cote® after my top surgery, with amazing results, and therefore I decided to use it again for my incision lines post-phallo.

The most exciting thing to happen this week was salt bathing my arm graft as Katie had instructed. Actually, it was the most

disgusting fun I've had since I was ten years old and fell off my bike. Being allowed to help the scabs come off is awesome. Not picking them, of course, but allowing the salt water to lift off the flaky bits and gently rubbing the skin to help. It was amazing to see it all come away and reveal gorgeous, pink, new skin. It was so good to see that the graft had taken well and, apart from a few stubborn areas, was healing well too.

I had been stepping up the arm exercises to include more wrist rotations and spending much more time not wearing the giant foam sling. The arm and hand were now much more mobile and I was beginning to use them more normally, although at this point I still couldn't straighten them fully and they felt much weaker than my other hand and arm. Sensation was also returning to my thumb and the area around it, which was a relief.

The only issue with using the hand more was the swelling. Some days my hand was huge, like a giant purple match-head on a stick. I bought myself a smaller, fabric sling, so that I could more easily keep it on but could repeatedly get my arm out and use it. I had to balance using the arm with then elevating it, to keep on top of the swelling.

I decided, after hearing good reviews, to try a compression glove. They are used for any condition that causes swelling in the hand, and they improve circulation too. I wore it through the night as that's when my hand swelled the most, and it helped.

The Long Recovery

Two to Six Months Post-Op

I knew that stage one would be a long, hard road to recovery, and I had accounted for that. However, as previously mentioned, by far the most surprising thing in my surgery recovery was how much I worried. I can be very positive and rational about the ups and downs of life, so to find myself in a constant state of concern was most unexpected.

Every day with surgery recovery seemed to bring a new concern. Nothing went massively wrong, but it was all the little stuff: the oozing, the stitches opening up a little, and worrying about every bend and crease in my new penis. I am incredibly grateful for the community of trans people who were willing to listen to my concerns and reassure me that everything would be okay.

The over-worrying is normal and it makes sense. Going through phalloplasty requires a huge investment in time, so the idea of something going wrong is utterly devastating. Also, there are so many unknown factors in surgery recovery. Although you are given rough guidelines of what to expect, people and bodies differ greatly and therefore so does the healing journey. There are

also so many areas of the body to look after, and each area has the potential to have all different kinds of healing complications. With all of this, it's impossible to know what your individual recovery will look like and prepare accordingly.

Again, I am going to note the similarities between phalloplasty and having a new baby, because it is so fitting. You are discharged from the hospital with a brand-new addition that you need to care for. You've spoken to people about their experience, you've done your research, you've bought everything in the suggested kit, but when you bring your new addition home, the reality is entirely different. It needs constant care, constant checking on and, as an individual, it has its own patterns and needs. Alex and I, like many new parents, were having to make it up as we went along. Should it smell like that? Should that be leaking? Is this the right way to put the dressing on? It is no wonder that this journey is marked with a lot of stress and worry. However, things did get easier as the weeks went by. Alex and I became more confident in how to look after Finn Jr.; and the more I healed, the less we worried.

Luckily, I am someone who heals fast. I do, however, also make sure to take really good care of myself after surgeries. Being in recovery means that I don't drink alcohol. Alcohol, especially too much of it, can really slow down healing. Other things I do to help myself is to take extra vitamin C and zinc. I swear by the dissolvable tablets that make a drink – that way, you stay hydrated and vitamin-nourished. Additionally, I take extra protein after surgery. I make sure to get as much protein-rich food as I can, but I also use a protein powder supplement and have that as a drink. I did lots of research on supplements that are said to aid healing and recovery. However, if you have any concerns you should always check with a doctor or nutritionist.

Two months post-op

By two months post-op, I had begun to feel more like my usual self. I needed to return to my studies but was very glad that I could do so from home. I could still get tired easily and my brain wasn't yet firing on all cylinders. I often found it very hard to concentrate and absorb the information. I made sure to just take it slowly and to study in short, manageable chunks. Really, two months is still incredibly early days, especially in the first stage of phalloplasty.

Finn Jr. continued to get much softer to the touch. He still felt quite heavy, but the swelling was considerably less. I now felt confident to let him hang freely, without panicking about him falling off. He seemed to be longer so I measured him to check. It turned out he had gained half an inch and was now 5½ inches long – maybe gravity had helped. The bend I had been seeing had disappeared; it had clearly been just swelling.

It was the most wonderful relief that by two months all of the weepy areas had finally dried up. The annoying area between my ball and groin was finally healed. Everything between my legs still felt delicate – not sore but not entirely comfortable either. I could walk fine, even without a waddle, but it was still impossible to wear jeans. I only wore loosely fitting jogging bottoms, for comfort and room. Having clothes on often caused sweating and irritation, so I used a bit of barrier cream around my groin area, just to stop any soreness. My new testicle was still quite delicate too. With hair constantly growing, one area between my ball and groin felt prickly. I have had issues with ingrowing hairs many times since then. Being a very hairy guy is problematic in lower surgery, that's for sure.

The healing of my arm was incredible. By the time I was two

months post-op, there was just one small area, about the size of a large bottle cap, which didn't seem to have taken. This is a common issue with grafts and can cause some scarring, rather than neat, new, pink skin. However, in the grand scheme of things it was a tiny issue compared with the overall impressive healing of my arm. I also noticed a small lump near the crook of my elbow at the edge of the scar. I asked Mr Stephens about it in an email and he said that it would settle in time.

At two months I also began to massage my arm twice daily. This is something I did with my top surgery scars and I have wonderful scar lines, so I repeated the same routine with my lower surgery scars. It's basically just to keep the new skin moisturized and supple. My favourite oil is tamanu oil and I always recommend that to trans folk. If the smell is too strong for you, you can always mix it with rosehip seed oil. Both these oils are said to have great healing properties. More than anything, though, it's the massage and moisture which help to keep the scar supple and thus heal better.

The use of my arm came back slowly. In the early days I was worried that my arm would never be the same again. However, like with the skin healing, my arm function surprised me. By two months I was getting much more movement in the hand, although the grip was still weak. Rotating the arm and wrist was still painful and I was doing it very gradually as part of my daily arm exercises. My arm made some strange noises when moving. I would get a disturbing loud 'clonk' when I tried to rotate the whole arm. By two months I had also completely stopped using a sling. This helped with strengthening my arm as I was using it more normally. However, as my arm was now not elevated, it did begin to swell a lot. I made sure to elevate the arm whenever I was sitting still, just to help the swelling go down. I used a compression glove when I was out and about, to help with the

swelling in my hand. I also covered my arm with a loose support bandage, to protect the skin.

The buttock incisions were also beginning to heal nicely. By two months post-op the incisions were becoming far more comfortable. I could now sit easily and was walking much better. The incision lines were still quite tight, which restricted my movement, especially when I tried to bend. I meditate, and at two months I was able to sit cross-legged for brief periods, but it still wasn't entirely comfortable. The area beneath my cheeks was still very numb to the touch. The incisions remained purple. Like with the arm, once the incision lines were fully healed and there were no oozy areas, I began massaging them with tamanu oil twice a day. Over time, like with my other scars, these would lighten in colour.

Three months post-op

By three months post-op, I had totally fallen in love with my penis. Up until that point I had been so focused on healing that the enormity of my changed body hadn't really sunk in. Now that everything was healed and nothing was leaking, my penis stopped being a surgical site. My view shifted from caring for him to bonding with him.

Finn Jr. now looked like a penis rather than a fat, overly cooked sausage. Okay, he still didn't have the glans (the head of the penis), so he wasn't entirely the correct shape, but without the swelling he looked so much better. Also, now that all the swelling had gone, I could let him hang without it causing me pain, and he was soft and malleable.

Although I couldn't yet feel anything in my penis, I could feel him on me, and the sensation of walking and feeling my penis

shift around in my pants was incredible. I loved feeling him swing between my legs as I walked. One of the most wonderful things at night was to roll onto my side and feel his weight as he moved and slapped against my thigh. I often woke and grinned when that happened. And how magnificent it was to be able to sleep on my side again. I am someone who really struggles to sleep on my back, so finally being able to side sleep meant I could sleep properly.

I thought, even at this very basic stage, that Finn Jr. was a very handsome penis. I knew, of course, that he would look even better once the glans was created and he had his own shiny new helmet. But even the way he looked in his basic form was incredibly gender-affirming. I loved to stand in the mirror and stare. I loved the way my body now looked completely whole with my new penis hanging exactly where it should be.

The area underneath my penis, however, was now a confusing mess. I still had my vagina. My T-dick had been stripped back. I had the beginning of an opening for urethral lengthening. I had one testicle, created by inserting an implant into one of the labia. The other labia remained the same. All this mess was hiding behind my beautiful penis, reminding me of how early in the journey I still was. For the first time, I was aware of how wet that area was, and it repulsed me in a way it hadn't before surgery. I couldn't wait to have it all closed down so that the area would be dry and my testicle would feel like a testicle rather than a repurposed labia. It was clear to me at this point that of course I wanted the Batcave closed. So much of this journey is impossible to know until you walk it. Now, seeing my penis, I knew I needed all trace of my old parts gone as they, in comparison with how right my penis felt, were so wrong.

By three months post-op, I had also begun to experiment with my new penis – very gently of course. I was relieved to

discover that none of the feeling in my old parts or my T-dick had changed at all. I managed to orgasm easily, using my T-dick. What I really wanted to try was penetrative sex. I had heard of other trans people having some luck using two condoms, to make their penis hard enough. I tried everything, two condoms, a loose bandage and a penis sleeve. None of these methods was very successful, but I had fun trying. The main reason they didn't work was because I was so worried about hurting Finn Jr. I couldn't feel any sensation yet, so I didn't know if what I was doing was too tight or hurting him. However, the good news was that all my old parts still worked. The most wonderful thing was that I could hold my new penis and then rub back and forth over my T-dick, so it was as though I was wanking like any other chap. Even though the actual route to an orgasm was still through my old equipment, the fact that I was holding my new penis whilst doing so was electrifying.

At just over three months post-op, finally, the one area of stubborn scab on my arm finally came off. The area was very deep and so the scab was thick. This wasn't helping the healing as it was coming away at the edges and in my pressing it back down to keep it flat, it was just staying wet underneath. I eventually trimmed it off carefully with scissors and after that it healed much better. The skin on the graft looked healthy. It was still very blotchy, but the colour was beginning to even out. The outline of the graft was healing nicely, helped by the massage. I also began to use Kelo-Cote® on some of the more raised and purple bits of the scar outline.

The swelling in both the arm and hand continued to decrease. By three months post-op I could let the arm hang more, without the hand going blue and swelling. The lump in the crook of my elbow remained but was significantly smaller. I stopped using the compression glove and the support bandage. Although these

had seemed to help initially, I noticed that they suddenly seemed to be making things worse. Soon after stopping using them, my swelling decreased again. I find that these things are very much trial and error. What works one week suddenly doesn't work the next. It's worth experimenting and trying out what works for you.

Not wearing a cover on my arm did cause me to worry, especially after an incident where I knocked my arm, only lightly, against a door frame and a blood blister appeared. I decided then to search for something lighter I could use to protect my arm without aggravating the swelling. I found some tattoo sleeve coverings, and these worked perfectly.

Movement of the arm by three months had also significantly improved. Although my fingers were still stiff, I could now fully straighten and rotate the arm without any pain, though the clonking sound was still there. The strangest thing was how alien my arm felt. It remained numb apart from a few areas where I could feel a tiny bit of touch and pressure. It felt odd, as if something tight was wrapped around it – not painful, but like wearing a tight bandage.

The area below my bum cheeks was now also steadily healing. At three months, I noticed some feeling returning in the skin there and it didn't feel as numb as it once had. However, this also meant that at times it got a bit sore from sitting on it. Movement could sometimes still be a little tricky too, mainly because the incision line was still really tight and when I stretched or bent it felt sore. Also, my tummy still felt a little bruised, just where the incision line went across my pubic bone and down into my groin. This meant bending was still difficult. I also had one problematic area where the scar line curved around from my bum to in my groin area. The scar line there was a bit puckered, and the extra skin meant it could get itchy at times. The scar line was also still

pretty purple. This was expected at this point, of course. Scars take a while to turn from purple to pink to white. The scar had also stretched and was quite wide, but that can't be helped really as that area stretches so much. I tried to spend as much time as I could massaging the area. Massaging your own arse is easier said than done. I also attempted to use a bit of Kelo-Cote® on some of the more problematic and raised bits of the scar line. All the other incisions were now fully healed, even the area that came open above the penis. Luckily, the hair began to grow back, and I could see that over time that scar would be covered.

Four months post-op

Reaching four months post-op, things began to get extremely exciting, as the first signs of sensation in my new penis arrived. Initially, the sensation I felt was very subtle, and it was also very strange. I first noticed the faint tingling of sensation when I was using my beard trimmer. First, I need to explain why I was using a beard trimmer on my penis. Unfortunately, the laser hair removal had not worked sufficiently. By four months post-op, I had significant hair regrowth. Although my penis wasn't as hairy as my arm, it did have an obvious furry coat. It seems that for hair removal to fully work, you need many more sessions than I'd had. In retrospect, I should have started hair removal at least a year before stage one. However, I wasn't overly worried about needing to shave my penis. Besides, the hair removal on my arm wouldn't have solved everything anyway. Because the scrotum is created using the labia, this means that you end up with a hairy nutsack, and I would have to trim that too. I believe the best way forward (unless you need the underneath of your forearm to be hair-free for the urethra) is to just wait until after

surgery is complete, and then have hair removal. That way, you can see exactly which areas need to be treated. However, I really didn't mind just trimming my penis and balls every week with a trimmer.

Anyway, trimming is what led me to excitedly discover that I had the very beginnings of sensation. When I touched my newly created penis with the trimmer, I could feel its vibration. Strangely, though, I didn't feel this sensation on my penis, but rather in my T-dick. This was rather surprising but apparently not uncommon. To explain, when the donor skin is taken from the forearm, they also harvest a couple of nerves. The harvested nerves are then placed through the newly created penis and attached to the back of the clitoris hood. Over time, these nerves regrow to give sensation. The displaced sensation I was experiencing, therefore, was the nerves regrowing, but the signals had not yet quite rewired properly. This was very promising, and I was very excited, in more ways than one.

At four months my arm was at last completely scab-free. A few stray hairs also began to appear. With double-thickness grafts, hair can regrow, but it usually isn't much. The arm was still very blotchy and discoloured, but that was to be expected in such early days.

The lump near my elbow crease had shrunk to just the tiniest of bumps, and all swelling had pretty much gone. I still got a bit of swelling above the incision line, below my wrist and into the hand a little, but it didn't balloon there like it had done in earlier months. I could walk with my hand down without it swelling. The lack of swelling meant that, at last, my hand looked like a normal hand for the first time since surgery.

Movement in the arm felt almost normal by four months and the clonking sound disappeared. I returned to exercise at this point and could weight-bear on the wrist. It needed lots of strengthening but this was a great start. My grip was gradually

increasing but still weak. When I made a fist, my fingers and hand ached. I knew that it was going to take time and I wasn't overly concerned. All in all, at four months post-op, I felt like I had made amazing progress.

I also noticed a strange thing beginning to happen to my hand at four months post-op. The back of my left hand was becoming excessively hairy. I hadn't had much hair there before and my right hand had very little. However, my left hand now had a fairly thick covering. I also noticed that lumps had started to form on my nails. It looked as if my nails were growing additional layers on top. On massaging my hand one day, loads of skin also began to shed from the skin on my hand. I couldn't find any information on why this happened. I concluded that it must have been the way my body was producing cells to repair itself. As my arm was injured, my body must have been over-producing repair cells on that side, causing thicker nails and excess hair and skin. Once I massaged the excess skin off, it was fine. Just a little gross.

My overall movement at four months post-op was steadily improving. Doing shoelaces up was tricky as my bum incisions were still tight and so bending was still very difficult, but all in all I could see a marked improvement. I could far more easily sit cross-legged. It was straightening my legs fully which caused the most problems. The skin remained sore and itchy at times. Hair was beginning to regrow in this area too, which wasn't helping with the itching at all.

Five months post-op

At five months post-op, at last I was able to begin to exercise normally. I returned to swimming and yoga and didn't have any problems at all. The only issue I had at this point, which I really

didn't mind, was where to place my penis. In trunks now, my bulge was obvious. I absolutely loved that I had a sizable bulge that was my own and not a prosthetic penis. However, I had to learn to be able to subtly shift Finn Jr. around when getting out of the pool, so that I didn't look as if I enjoyed swimming too much. I had similar issues with yoga. I discovered that I could no longer do certain poses without my penis getting in the way. These, of course, were all very enjoyable issues.

In terms of physical limitations, I could feel that my left wrist was still weaker than my right, but I could weight-bear much better by this point. The yoga also really helped to loosen the bum incisions, which at times still felt tight. The incision lines were now really stretched, but because of where they were, this was unavoidable. I hoped that as they faded to white, they would look better. The incision line between my legs was still quite itchy. There was still a lot of puckering and excess skin there. I had been told this all might take time to settle and there was the option of having things tidied up later on if it was problematic. I just massaged the area as best I could and continued with gentle exercise.

The colour on my arm began to fade more as I persevered with the same massage routine. I began to find that the skin on my graft arm would get drier more quickly, so I began to carry a small pot of moisturizer with me during the day to keep the arm from feeling too tight. I still covered my arm at this point, using the thin tattoo sleeves I found online.

Six months post-op

The sensation in my new penis continued to get stronger. By six months post-op, the feeling had become far more definite – in

fact, incredibly sensitive. The sensitivity was very much like when my T-dick first began to grow and anything touching it would make me hit the ceiling. At around six months post-op, I also began to feel a second displaced feeling. Now when I touched my new penis, I not only felt it in my T-dick but also in my groin area. Again, this made sense as one of the harvested nerves had been joined somewhere in the lower abdomen. This new sensation was clearly because a new nerve connection was beginning to wake up and regrow. To reach climax at this point, I still needed to directly stimulate my T-dick because there was not enough sensation in my new penis yet. However, by this point, touching my new penis had become pleasurable, and I began to incorporate playing with it at the same time as stimulating my T-dick.

By six months post-op, my arm was vastly improved. The colour of the skin on my arm was becoming much more even and closer to the normal skin tone of the rest of my arm. I also noticed a few more hairs appearing on the arm – just a few random patches and tufts. The skin on my arm still felt tight but I was getting used to the odd feeling by now. There was still little sensation in the arm. By now, my arm was pretty much back to how it had been, except for a little bit of stiffness in the hand. It was worse first thing in the morning, but after doing some hand exercises it would loosen up. The only thing that seemed entirely changed was my fine motor grip. I noticed this one morning on attempting to open a yoghurt pot. But, in the grand scheme of things, opening a yoghurt with my left hand is a loss I was willing to accept.

By six months all my incisions had healed incredibly well. My bum incisions were so much more supple. Although there was still a fair amount of puckering at the outer edge of the scar line and in my groin area, I knew it was early days and it could be

tidied up later if necessary. The main issue was that it caused a lot of itching. Cooped up in pants and trousers didn't help, so I tried to spend time naked and let everything get some fresh air.

The incisions on my tummy going down into my groin were healing nicely and beginning to fade. The incision which had opened on my pubic area had now healed too. However, this scar was wide and purple, and since no hair was growing on it, it wouldn't be well hidden. I wasn't happy with how it looked but I knew that it would fade in time. Unfortunately, scars are a part of the process, but then only me and my partner would see them. I remember that it took until about six months after my top surgery for a real difference to be seen in those scars. Now, my top surgery scars look great, so I remained optimistic about my lower surgery scars.

Preparing for stage two phalloplasty

By six months post-op, I was ready to go ahead with stage two. I knew I could expect a surgery date any time soon. I had seen Mr Stephens for a post-op consultation when I was two months post-op. He was pleased with my healing and was happy to put me on the waiting list for stage two. St Peter's will only list you for your next stage if your healing is going to plan. At that time, however, I felt nowhere near ready for more surgery. My body may have physically healed, but mentally I was only just recovering. The first stage of lower surgery had been incredibly draining. But I knew I wouldn't likely get a surgery date for a few months, so I'd agreed to be put on the list.

Before I started my surgery, I had hoped that the three months' wait between surgery stages was correct. I liked the idea of getting things done quickly. However, having had my first

stage, I was very grateful that the actual wait between stages was longer than three months. Had it not been, I would have postponed any further surgery because I just wasn't ready before six months. Stage one took everything out of me and there were many times, when the healing was slow and the pain level high, that I wondered what on earth I had started. By six months, I had regathered all my mental resolve and felt strong enough to go through surgery again. Although I was not looking forward to more surgery and pain, I was looking forward to having things finished off. Having a strange area between your legs under a penis is a very odd thing. I was also looking forward to being able to pee standing up.

Expecting a date any time, I also needed to make my mind up, fast, about the decisions I had so far put off. At stage two, I would have the option of the vaginectomy to consider, as well as deciding whether to bury my T-dick. The vaginectomy was now an easy choice. I began to understand what I had read in *Hung Jury* about the difference between having a wet area versus a dry area. Suddenly, the damp opening beneath my penis was a huge source of dysphoria. In many ways, my dysphoria had increased in some areas and that was one of them. This was very much like the awakening I had when I realized I needed a penis. Once I realized how right my genitals looked with the correct parts, the old parts suddenly became a source of huge distress.

Dysphoria is a strange thing. It often doesn't present as a whole – at least, it didn't for me. My dysphoria became more and more fragmented as my transition progressed. What I mean by this is that initially I experienced dysphoria as one entity related to my gender incongruence. Then as I began to understand my distress and make sense of it, I realized that certain aspects of me had different levels of dysphoria. These levels of dysphoria have changed over time as my body has changed. The more correct

certain parts of me became, such as my voice on testosterone and my flat chest, the louder and more painful other parts of the dysphoria became. At six months post-lower surgery, I had huge gender euphoria at having my new penis, but other aspects of my lower dysphoria had become far worse. I now had huge levels of dysphoria about my vagina, which in many ways had not been there before. My penis was magnificent, and it felt so right. Now, in comparison, everything left behind underneath was so incredibly wrong. I was now eager to have the Batcave closed for business and have the entire area dry, as it now felt it should be.

Deciding whether to bury my T-dick, however, was now even harder to work out. I talked this through with Mr Bruno, to help me answer some of my questions and concerns. My main concern was about any complications to the urethral hook-up at stage two resulting from the placement of my T-dick. If there had been, then I would have been led by that as I was willing to do whatever it took to have a successful outcome of urethral lengthening. Mr Bruno said that it made no difference either way as it was just a case of whether to close skin over the top of the T-dick or not. It was good to know that there were no medical complications, but now that meant that the decision was down to me.

My instinct was to choose burial. Everything looked a jumbled mess between my legs. And like with the vaginectomy, all I wanted was it to be neat and tidy. I couldn't imagine what it would look like, with everything closed and just the head of my stripped back T dick poking out. Suddenly, in having this beautiful penis, the other, non-male-specific parts looked completely out of place.

I no longer had the same attachment to my T-dick as I'd had pre-surgery. It no longer seemed to be this beautiful thing I had

grown. It might well be able to get its own erections and look like a perfectly crafted mini-penis but now, in comparison with the real thing, I did not love it in the same way at all.

The only reason I was struggling with this decision was because I was concerned about sensation. At just six months post-op, I only had the very beginnings of sensation in my new penis and I still had to use my T-dick to achieve an orgasm. I was worried that if I buried it, I wouldn't be able to find it to orgasm with. I hoped that, one day, I wouldn't need to rely on my T-dick to orgasm. However, I couldn't guarantee that outcome. The idea of having this wonderful new penis, but no ability to orgasm, terrified the hell out of me.

The hardest part in making the decision was the need to base it on guesswork. In an ideal situation, I would wait, see what sensation returned, and decide from there. But it can take a year to 18 months for sensation to begin to return, and a couple of years for full sensation recovery to be achieved. I couldn't wait that long. Therefore, the only option was to take a complete gamble on whether to bury my T-dick and hope that I could either still access it or gain enough sensation in my new penis to not have to rely on it.

I spent lots of time chatting with kind trans guys willing to share their experiences. No one I spoke to said that orgasm was impossible, which was reassuring. And most people who had chosen burial could still easily locate the clitoris under the skin if they needed to. This was reassuring, but I was still afraid. What if I was the rare one who chose burial and could neither find my buried T-dick nor manage to reach orgasm with my new penis?

The other option was to leave it unburied, see how things progressed and if sensation returned, bury it later. But I really didn't like the idea of that. I just wanted everything tidy right now. I also didn't like the thought of having a new penis but

still having to rely on my old equipment to get off. Just the thought of that made my dysphoria burn brightly in my gut. I had to accept, though, that I might not get enough sensation in my new penis to rely completely on an orgasm that way. At six months post-op, the early signs were promising, but I still had to manage my expectations.

When I had spoken to Mr Bruno regarding the burial, he had said I could change my mind right up until the morning of surgery, so all I could do between now and then was keep weighing up the options and hope one of them made itself clear.

The Freedom of Standing to Pee

Stage Two Phalloplasty

I had only two days' notice when, in the following April of 2016, I received a date for the second stage of surgery. I had told St Peter's that I was available at short notice, but, still, when David rang on the Thursday, offering me a cancellation slot for the coming Saturday, it was a bit of a shock. Luckily, I had prepared everything, just in case this happened. In my experience, surgeries often happen this way – at short notice – so it is wise to have things prepared just in case. David had informed me that my surgery would again be performed by Mr Stephens, and I was very pleased about this. I loved my results from stage one and felt very confident in his ability. My surgery would be at the Spire Hospital in Slough again. This time, I was to be admitted on the day of the procedure rather than the night before. Stage two would involve a few different procedures. I would have a hysterectomy, vaginectomy, urethral lengthening and the glans of my penis created.

At this point I was just over seven months post-op from stage one. I was ready for stage two now – in fact, I was desperate for it. Having my penis half-finished was really getting me down.

At first, the joy of having a new penis had been wonderful, and whilst that joy was still there, so were the reminders that I was far from being finished. Having to flush through my penis every day was getting tedious. Needing to lift my penis up and pop him on the toilet seat in front of me, whilst I sat to pee, was soul-crushing. I knew it was temporary, but dysphoria does not respond to logic.

Mentally, though, I wasn't in the best place for surgery at all. The timing would really impact on my degree studies, with exams coming up in June. Also, Alex and I were having some issues in our relationship. We had agreed to spend some time apart. We were still living together, but in different rooms. We hadn't fallen out at this point; we were still very much friends. Alex just needed some time to work out what he wanted. I could understand this. The combination of my transition and surgery, and then his transition and starting hormones, was a huge upheaval. I understood and respected his need for time. Alex said he would still help me through stage two, and I was very grateful for that. But, of course, I was sad, confused and worried as I didn't know if our relationship was ending.

With all this going on, although I was excited for surgery, I wasn't in the best place mentally to have it done; but I just needed to go ahead and get through it. Sometimes in this journey, it's about picking between two equally bad decisions. To have put off the surgery would have greatly impacted my dysphoria, so, either way, my mental health was going to take a hit. I just did my best to keep life simple. I arranged extensions for my essays and practised lots of self-care over the days leading up to surgery.

On the day of the surgery, I made my own way to Slough, using public transport. It wasn't too difficult for me to get to, being based in Oxford at the time. It was far less stressful being admitted on the day itself. It meant I could get a proper night's

sleep in my own bed the night before, and get myself showered and ready in my own home before heading to hospital. As my surgeries progressed, I took to using Hibiscrub® at home. It wasn't always given to me before surgery and I figured it was better to be safe than sorry. I wanted to give myself the best possible chance of a success because stage two carried the most risks of infection.

Arriving at the hospital, I was admitted and shown to my room. The nurses arrived to do all the usual observations: blood pressure, swabs, and so on. Mr Stephens visited and went over everything that was going to happen. He also wanted to confirm my choice of burial of the clitoris. By this point, I had decided to risk it and choose burial. I just wanted everything to look right. I felt reassured enough that I would still be able to access my T-dick in the meantime, until enough sensation returned to be able to orgasm with my new penis.

Soon after Mr Stephens left, the hysterectomy surgeon also visited to discuss the procedure. I had to sign the usual scary forms which outline the worst-case scenario of everything: risk of the urethra failing; risk of bleeding from the vaginectomy. These risks washed over my head. By this point, the desperate need to have my urethra hooked up, the Batcave closed, and all trace of my reproductive system gone made these complications mean nothing. I knew that complications happened and that people overcame them when they did, and that was all that mattered. Of course, I still hoped they wouldn't happen to me, but I had managed my expectations and prepared for any eventuality.

Having said that, I did feel far more nervous for stage two than I had for stage one. I think the memory of all the pain at stage one wasn't helping. Plus, I had just got used to the way my new body looked, felt and worked, and now here I was about

to have it all changed again. Of course, I wanted the changes, I wanted things tidy and I knew logically that each surgery was getting closer to that; but still, the nerves about surgery remained.

Finally, the door to my room swung open and in walked an incredibly tall man. His stature was exaggerated by the fact that he was all in blue, with one of those surgeon's caps that look like a cloth swim cap. He looked like a giant blue matchstick. This was my anaesthesiologist. As with stage one, I was asked to walk to theatre. This was just as odd as the first time, but things were about to get even stranger.

Arriving in the theatre pre-op room, the smiling matchstick man invited me to sit on the bed. I did as he asked and then watched as he and his team began organizing everything around me. The matchstick man placed a cannula in my hand, as usual, but this time, he injected me with... 'Something to help you to relax.'

Within minutes, I felt like I had smoked a loaded joint, which isn't good for an addict in recovery. I sat on the edge of the bed, off my face and chatting rubbish for a few minutes, whilst they all continued to ready the room. Surely now it was time to lie down, go to sleep, and wake up with a working pee pipe. No, apparently not.

Next the matchstick man explained that I was to have an injection in my back, to help with the pain post-op. I was instructed to stay seated but lean forward. A nurse then injected what I can only assume to be an epidural. I have never found out what it was and have never had one since. It was quick and it didn't hurt at all. Once done, the matchstick man quickly helped me to lift my legs onto the trolley bed and lie down. By now, I was feeling more off my face than I'd done since I got clean and sober in 2010. Finally, the matchstick man began the procedure

I was used to – where they put a mask on your face, inject you with something cold, and then the world disappears.

When I woke up, I honestly felt great. No surprise really, considering the medication party I'd had in the pre-op room. I was comfortable and pain-free – nothing like the awakening experience I'd had with stage one. I breathed a sigh of relief to feel okay and to be told that everything had gone well.

As I was wheeled back to my room, I was surprised to see that it was much later than I had expected. I was told the surgery should have been four hours. Mr Stephens explained that it had taken longer because they had found a problem: the part of my urethral tube that they had created at stage one had a narrowing. He used skin from my clitoris hood to fix it and said it should be fine. Apart from that, everything else had been straightforward and went well.

I was relieved it was all over and had gone okay. I let myself return to sleeping, or, more to the point, dozing in and out of a very drugged-up haze. I kept expecting the numbness to wear off and to feel pain, but I didn't. I managed to doze on and off all night without any pain whatsoever, right through until 6 o'clock the following morning.

Day 2 post-op

I was starving by the time I awoke the following morning, having been allowed water but no food. I had ordered a giant breakfast, and when it arrived I could have kissed the nurse with joy.

After breakfast, the nurse assisted me with a bed bath. This is when I discovered the only area of pain I seemed to have was right between my legs. Touching anywhere there, even lightly, hurt like hell and made everything internal start to spasm.

If it wasn't touched, the pain was fine. I managed to get a look at how everything was looking down there and take stock of all the new wounds. Finn Jr. looked good from what I could see. He had a cute blue bandage around his head, so I couldn't yet see the glans, but otherwise all looked okay. I had one dressing from the hysterectomy, where they did the keyhole procedure. I had a drain out of my side, which would be removed before I went home. The drain was just to make sure blood was coming out, rather than staying inside me, and there wasn't much blood in the drain. I also had a stent through my penis, which was like a catheter tube, only not connected to a bag. The stent was to keep the urethra open until it had healed enough to pee through. The catheter I had fitted was suprapubic, which means it goes directly into your bladder via a hole in the lower abdomen.

After helping me to wash, the nurse helped me to get up from the bed and onto a chair. I was wobbly, but other than that, moving was fine. Sitting was a bit painful at first, but it soon settled and I managed to stay in the chair all day rather than returning to the bed.

During the day, I was shown how to use the catheter. The nurse guided me through how to empty and change the bag, as I would have the catheter for ten days at home. The first attempt was quite tricky. The urine bag was strapped to my lower leg and I couldn't bend over very far. I called for the nurse, who showed me how to lift my leg and place one foot on the toilet basin; that way, I could undo the catheter valve and drain it. Bingo!

The physiotherapist visited too, just to make sure I was moving around okay. I was able to move quite easily. The main issue was bringing my drain with me. The physiotherapist was happy that I was mobile enough to go home. If everything continued okay, I would only be in for one more night.

At this point, the pain was still very minimal. I felt incredibly

bloated and my tummy was sore, but there was no real pain to speak of. The catheter was giving me some issues, though. I had the constant feeling that I needed to pee, which of course I didn't as I had a catheter. However, my bladder seemed to think otherwise. I mentioned this to the nurses a few times as I felt concerned. I was reassured that my bladder was just adjusting to the catheter and that it would settle. All in all, apart from these relatively minor things, stage two was so far a walk in the park compared with stage one. However, it didn't stay that way.

Recovering at home

The following morning, I was discharged and returned home. By the time I arrived, I was shattered but okay. The next day was when all the problems started.

The pain itself wasn't too bad at that stage, but the desire to pee was driving me round the bend. Although I had the catheter, I still felt as though I was bursting for the loo all the time. My urine was clear, I was drinking lots of clear fluids and the catheter was draining well, so there weren't any apparent issues. I asked around on the lower surgery forums for advice. I discovered that this irritation was a common symptom with catheters, especially suprapubic ones which go directly into the bladder.

What tends to cause the irritation is that there is a balloon on the end of the catheter tube inside your bladder. When this balloon touches the bladder wall, it can cause irritation and urge to pee. I think having the stent and the suprapubic catheter both going into my bladder, each with a balloon touching my bladder wall, was just too much irritation for my sensitive bladder to handle. I rang my local doctor, who prescribed oxybutynin,

which would help with bladder spasms and the urges to pee. I managed to waddle to the local pharmacy to pick it up, without too much of an issue.

By the following day, the medication did seem to be easing things a little. However, pain everywhere else had amplified. If I remained lying down, the pain was minimal. However, sitting up really hurt, and as soon as I stood upright, the pain became intense. I could now barely walk. With needing to walk to the toilet to empty the catheter quite frequently, I was in agony.

Unfortunately, I was having to go through this alone. Alex had decided to go away for a few days, so he wasn't with me for this surgery recovery. I was hurt and sad to lose his support, but I had agreed that the opportunity would likely help him to work through what was going on for him. I should, at this point, have reached out to friends to ask for help, but I was too embarrassed. I had not yet made it public, even with my friends, that Alex and I were having relationship difficulties, so I kept quiet and just got on with looking after myself as best I could.

Although the pain was intense, and in fact far more intense by this point than any pain had been at stage one, I could at least look after myself. I could manage to slowly wash myself, cook, and feed myself, so in many ways it was still easier than stage one.

One week post-op

The following Monday, I visited my local practice nurse. It was time to remove the stent from my penis and to check the dressing of the glans. I was looking forward to having the stent removed. I hoped that one less tube into my bladder might help to lessen the irritation. The oxybutynin was helping, but I was

still struggling with urges to pee and bladder pains. I was quite nervous about the penis stent coming out, but it was fine – a little odd but not painful at all. It felt good to be free of the tube.

I was also nervous about the dressing being removed from the glans. The blue gauze had been quite thickly taped. The nurse really struggled to undo it, and it was sticking to my penis. Bless the nurse, she was wincing on my behalf. At this point, I was glad about having only limited sensation in my penis. But it hurt more than I imagined it would, which I was also quite glad of. To notice more feeling was a great excitement, which made up for the pain.

I was surprised to see how clean my new glans looked. After having the arm graft, I was imagining the worst, but it looked almost healed already. There was just a bit of dried blood in the ridge, and the stitches needed to settle, but otherwise the new tip of my penis looked amazing.

After having the stent removed, I had much less trouble walking and a little less pain between my legs. I could now have my first proper shower, and having less pain helped a lot with this. My post-op notes said to put a fresh dressing on the glans every day until it was healed. However, my practice nurse said it was probably best to do it every two days, so as not to disturb the wound too much. I decided to follow her advice and stick with every other day.

My post-op appointment with St Peter's was done by telephone this time. The nurse just wanted to check everything was healing okay. I was pleased to report that all my wounds were fine. Everything was healing quickly. I'd had no bleeding from the vaginectomy site, which was a relief. The wound area underneath my penis was still swollen but slowly going down. The bruising was coming out more too, which was to be expected. An odd thing to note was that my stage one scars from the buttock

graft had swollen up. The nurse said it was likely just because everything else down there was swollen too.

Two weeks post-op

By two weeks post-op, I was still very sore, and my movement was restricted, but I began to see little improvements each day. I was still having difficulty walking but standing was far less excruciating than it had been.

All my wounds were now fabulously healed. However, changing the glans dressing was a nightmare. In the end, I decided that I would just leave it off. My glans had almost healed and I felt that messing with pulling the dressing off was not helping. Leaving it to air for a few days helped. My shiny new helmet looked amazing, even if it was a little battered. It was fantastic that my penis now looked more like a penis, rather than a sausage.

The catheter was still being incredibly annoying. The oxybutynin no longer seemed to be working at all and the urge to pee was driving me insane. I was up all night with urges to pee. If I moved in my sleep the catheter pulled and hurt like hell. And, I had found blood in my urine. A visit to my doctor confirmed I had a urine infection, and I was put on a course of antibiotics. I needed the infection gone by the following Tuesday when I was due to have the catheter removed and begin to start peeing through my penis. I wouldn't be able to start this if the infection was still present as it would risk damaging my new urethra.

The plan – in preparation for catheter removal – would be to replace the catheter bag with a flip-flow valve. This means that you are not free-draining into a bag, but instead emptying your bladder through the valve when the urge to pee comes.

When I explained this to a nurse friend, she suggested I ask if I could swap to the flip-flow early. It seemed that my bladder did not like catheters. Perhaps, if I could pee more normally, my bladder would stop getting irritated and infected. Keeping the bladder full can help to stop the balloon hitting the bladder wall. That's why it's recommended to drink plenty of clear fluids when you have a catheter. But still, having a bag would mean the bladder was constantly emptying, and this held more potential for irritation.

Desperate for an end to the catheter hell, I emailed Mr Stephens. He was happy for me to start using the flip-flow early, if I refrained from peeing through my penis, so I swapped it over. I noticed an immediate relief in the pain and the urge to pee. The remainder of the second week was far easier after that.

Three weeks post-op – toilet training begins

Reaching three weeks post-op meant that, at last, I could make my first attempt at peeing through my new urethra. In the UK they like to do this gradually, just to make sure everything is working okay. So, you keep the suprapubic catheter in for the first few days of learning to pee. My instructions were to pee through my penis; then, once I'd emptied as much as I could, I was to open the flip-flow valve, the aim being to completely empty my bladder so that very little urine came out via the suprapubic catheter. Once I was able to drain my bladder via my new urethra, I could have the catheter removed.

On the Monday of Week 3, I was a ball of nervous and excited energy and ready to give my first pee a try. I had been advised to attempt this in the shower as the first pee can be a bit of a spray. I drank a ton of water and waited for the urge to arrive.

Standing in the shower, my new penis in hand, I took a deep breath and let go of my bladder muscles. As I began to feel the sensation of letting go to pee, it felt as though it was going to come out from the old place, and I had to fight the urge to hold onto my wee. Then suddenly, a wide spray exploded from the end of my penis.

'I'm peeing!' I yelled to an empty flat as my pee spray began to go in every direction except straight forward. Then, I burst into floods of incredibly happy and relieved tears.

Having no issues with emptying my bladder, a couple of days later I visited my practice nurse to have the awful catheter removed. The nurse had a lot of difficulty getting it out, and it was incredibly painful, which shows how much everything was irritated in there.

In the days which followed, I mastered the art of aiming for the toilet. I was mostly successful, apart from the times where I forgot and instead sat down to pee, or sat down to do a poo and left my penis out in front of me, resting on the toilet seat, and then peed all over my feet. Toilet training as a fully grown adult proved to be quite the learning curve.

One month post-op

By one-month post-op, I felt pretty much back to my normal self. Overall, the recovery had been much easier compared with stage one. I would describe stage two as the most intensely painful but also the quickest recovery. Using the new baby analogy again, once you are holding your newborn in your hand, all the pain, no matter how intense, pales into insignificance.

I was peeing without any issues whatsoever. I still had the

odd bit of stinging when using the toilet, but no other pain at all. I'd heard some other trans guys mention that they had a bit of dripping after peeing. Many said that they had to really work on 'milking' their penis (goodness, I wish there was a better term for that) to get the last drops out. I didn't seem to have that issue at all. I noticed that if I pushed on the very base of my penis, a few more drips came out, so I did that instead.

I took great joy in heading out to town and visiting lots of different cafés, so that I could try out as many different urinals as possible. I was like the wolf marking his territory as I peed all over my local land. I didn't have any problem using urinals; there was no bladder shyness. I think because I had used a stand-to-pee device before surgery, I was already used to peeing in public, so that hurdle had already been jumped over. It was incredibly liberating to be able to use a urinal. It was especially a relief to not have the fear of people noticing that my penis was silicone or worrying about back flow. The strange sensation that my pee was going to come from the old place remained, but I got used to that feeling. I did need to get my entire penis out to pee. Again, the issue is that we are showers not growers (i.e. the penis is always the same length), and I just couldn't get him through my fly because of his size. It was easy, though, to just undo my button, a bit of my zip, and then pull Finn Jr. out over the top of my pants. Now I just had to master the technique of how many shakes of a penis was socially appropriate. Toilet etiquette is a funny thing. I worried about it a little in the early days, but after seeing the way some men behave at a urinal, I stopped worrying.

The freedom of being able to pee had such a positive impact on my mental wellbeing. My anxiety levels already made it challenging to go out in public. The concern about using toilets had made that even more difficult. However, after the second stage,

going out was far less of an issue now that toilets were no longer a concern. This new freedom was wonderful and liberating in so many ways. I saw a marked decrease in my social anxiety.

Everything else had healed and I felt in good spirits. I recovered far more quickly emotionally from stage two than I did from stage one. With the hysterectomy done, I had been prepared to feel a bit emotionally unstable. I thought it might knock my hormones off-balance and affect my mood. However, it didn't seem to do that at all. More than anything, I was pleased to no longer be experiencing period-like cramps.

I was incredibly lucky with the way the vaginectomy site healed. I had no bleeding from there at all. The way they performed the vaginectomy in the UK at the time of my surgery was to use cauterization. This was said to be much safer than the old method of removing the lining of the vagina. Cauterization meant that sometimes you could have post-op bleeding. Just the thought of blood coming from there, even though I knew it wasn't period blood, was enough to spark a dysphoric meltdown. Luckily, I didn't have to deal with that.

With my uncertainties around the vaginectomy pre-stage one, I had expected to feel the loss of the Batcave. However, having everything closed felt incredibly normal. It was also a delight to have a dry area and a dry ball underneath my penis. Mr Stephens had made a start on the scrotoplasty. I'd had my first testicle implant at the first stage. Now I had been tidied up and my other labia remained as an empty sack, ready for the pump device at stage three. There was still work to be done, but already things looked much neater.

My penis was looking wonderful. I had been concerned about how my self-harm scars might impact the glansplasty. I did have the white scars on the end of my penis, so my knob end looked wrinkly rather than the smooth, domed appearance of most

glans. However, I didn't mind, and I was just happy to have a knob. The graft for my glans was taken from my left side by my hip. By a month post-op, it was still very purple and quite itchy but otherwise fine.

By a month post-op, the swelling underneath my penis had gone down. Then, it was possible to have a feel and see if I could still locate my T-dick. I was relieved to find I could easily feel it under the skin, and that the entire area there had full sensation. I had my first very gentle play at a month post-op, and, to my relief, I could still orgasm. I was glad I had chosen burial as it added to the tidiness under my penis and had not impacted my ability to orgasm at all.

Three months post-op (and one year from stage one)

At three months post-op from stage two, I also turned a year post-op from stage one. I marvelled at how far I'd come and how well I had healed. My penis was an hourly delight. Whether I was moving and felt my penis shift and felt his warmth on my leg, or whether I was holding him to pee, I wore a constant euphoric grin of joy. Finn Jr. looked amazing to me. I couldn't believe anybody could ever describe the results of phalloplasty as a Frankenstein monster. Even with owner bias, my penis was anything but a monster.

The self-harm scars from my arm were visible on my penis. However, the main ones were on the underside and therefore hidden. The other scars around my knob were on show but they didn't bother me at all. I felt that these scars just made my penis uniquely mine. Having only one ball was no longer an issue – I could live with that, now that the underneath was tidy.

Sensation had continued to return. I had been fearful that after stage two I might lose the sensation I had gained after stage one, but that hadn't happened. The sensation was still patchy and displaced but it was increasing all the time.

My ability to orgasm hadn't been affected by either the burial of my T-dick or the vaginectomy. Because the vaginectomy doesn't remove the vagina but cauterizes it instead, the muscles which remain still play a part in an orgasm. My orgasms after stage two were far more intense, and I wonder if that's because the muscles contract differently once they've been closed in. Whatever it was, I was pleased with the outcome.

I was pleased too that even with my T-dick buried, I could still feel when it got erect. The most incredible thing about burial is that it changed the way I wanked. Because I had full sensation underneath my penis, where my hand hit the base in a back-and-forward motion, it hit the area where my T-dick was buried, and I could achieve orgasm that way. This was an awesome development. Being able to wank like any other man, without having to rely directly on my T-dick to come, helped to further decrease my dysphoria. I hadn't considered this was an option at all. It's tricky trying to imagine how sensation will show up. And this new development was a welcome surprise. Okay, I was still sort of relying on my T-dick being stimulated to orgasm, but it was in a non-direct way, and so didn't matter to me. I felt relief that even if I didn't get full sensation in my penis, I could at least still orgasm with just my new penis.

Everything else was healing amazingly well too. All the scars, from both stage one and two, were beginning to fade. My arm was changing into a more even colour. I was very careful to not get it in the sun and used a sunblock to protect the graft. It did still tan a bit, but this improved the colour and look of the scar. The arm and hand were now functioning normally, although

weight-bearing on my wrist could sometimes be difficult when I was exercising.

My bum incisions were taking longer than everything else to heal but they were in a difficult area to look after. The scars were increasingly more stretched and still very purple. And, at times, the area could still feel tight when bending, or sore after sitting for a while.

Six months post-op

The most significant changes leading up to six months post-op were the psychological ones. Stage two had made an enormous difference to my life in being incredibly gender-affirming. Although I had placed little significance on the hysterectomy, and had been hesitant about having the vaginectomy, knowing I no longer had any female parts was incredibly gender-affirming. Being able to stand to pee had made me grow in self-confidence. The simple freedom of being able to wander into a toilet and pee like any other man opened up whole new areas in my life. I was no longer afraid in social situations. I didn't have to stress about where I was going to pee when I went out. In the place of dysphoria there was this enormous space of inner peace. Having a finished penis, complete with his brand-new tip, was an immense joy. I no longer felt in limbo and half-finished, even though, of course, there was still a final stage to be done. Even without the erectile device, I already felt more complete and at home in my body than I had ever thought possible.

Reaching six months post-op was also a relief because I had no issues with urination. It's common for strictures or fistulas to appear in the first few months. Making it to six months issue-free meant I could at last relax. I was still very careful, though,

to drink plenty of water and avoid caffeine as much as possible. I felt very lucky as stage two is often the one with the most complications.

So far, my surgery had been straightforward. How much of that was luck and how much was my attention to looking after myself, I don't know. However, like I mentioned earlier, through my surgeries I eat healthily (even if I am not the world's best cook). I don't smoke and I don't drink alcohol. I drink a ton of water and I take high doses of vitamin C and zinc. I do what I am told. I rest, I meditate, and I think positive thoughts (there is a large amount of research showing the tangible effects of positive thinking). However, even people who do everything right can end up with problems. Therefore, I think it's part looking after myself well, part body genetics, and part luck.

The success of stage two was an enormous blessing for me. My dysphoria had been the worst in relation to having to sit to pee. The elation at finally being able to pee through my own flesh was euphoric. My joy at the success of stage two was also a blessing, because the rest of my life was rapidly falling apart.

The issues between Alex and me had finally come to a head. Alex confirmed my suspicions and admitted he had met someone else. He had met up with an ex-partner and they wanted to begin a relationship. This was a very surreal and devastating fact to get my head around. I had expected that it would be transition or surgery which would cause our relationship to come to an end. After all we had been through – Alex adjusting to my being trans, and then me adjusting to him coming out – to have the relationship end like this was a huge blow. The biggest upset, though, was the loss of our friendship. Alex and I had been so close. Through all the ups and downs and through the trial separation there had been no malice. We both just wanted the best for each other. We had already promised each other that,

if either of us chose to end the relationship, there would be no blame. But I still felt hurt and angry. Not only had I lost a partner, I had also lost my best friend.

I decided that the end of the relationship was my chance to start afresh. I no longer had to work through my issues around being gay, because I was no longer with a man. I could move somewhere new, where nobody knew my past. I could have some time on my own and get to know myself, independent of anyone else. Then, further down the line, I could return to dating and meet a wonderful woman to settle down with. Oh, how I laugh when I recall thinking this now.

A Failed Attempt at Stage Three and a Giant Step Backwards

The summer came and went as I waited as patiently as I could for stage three. Luckily, I had lots to keep me busy. Alex and I had separated, and I had left Oxford. With my gender clinic in Devon, along with possibilities for volunteer work and friends based in the area, it was the logical place to move to. I had settled into a cosy flat in the beautifully quaint and peaceful seaside town of Dawlish in Devon. The burn of losing Alex had faded. I was no longer angry about the way it had ended, we had grown apart anyway, and I was enjoying being my own man. Life was good.

Christmas arrived, and with it finally a date for stage three. St Peter's rang me on the 20th December, to give me a surgery date for the 13th January the following year. That was the most notice I had been given for a surgery date. This time, the surgery would be with Mr Bruno, at St John & St Elizabeth Hospital in London. The news of a date made looking ahead to 2017 exciting indeed. To see the finish line so close was thrilling.

I'd had an appointment with Mr Stephens before I left Oxford, to discuss erectile devices. At the time of my surgery, the UK offered the choice of an inflatable device or a malleable rod.

I had already ruled out the rod. I didn't like the idea that I would have a static penis. One of my biggest joys was my penis moving in my pants and swinging as I walked. The malleable rod would have to be bent erect and bent flaccid, meaning my penis would always be stiff and not hang free.

The inflatable device would give me the nearest thing to a natural erection. The inflatable device has three parts: a reservoir in the abdomen containing saline solution, a pump device in the scrotum, and a cylinder in the penis. The pump, placed as one of my testicles, would pump the solution from the reservoir into the cylinder in my penis, giving me an erection. A button on the pump device would release the saline solution from the cylinder back into the reservoir. When deflated, therefore, my penis would hang freely. I know some guys have concerns about having a mechanical device inside their bodies, but for me this was never an issue. I was excited at the thought of being able to use a pump to get erect, even if it was mechanically assisted.

The issue I *was* concerned about, however, was the life of the pump. They last on average five to ten years before they need to be replaced. The malleable rod, however, can last for upwards of 20 years before a replacement is needed. It still wasn't enough for me to want the rod, though.

My thought process was that if erectile devices improved, which they were likely to do by the time I needed mine replacing, then at least I could upgrade when the time came. Based on my age, I would be looking at a refitting in my late forties to early fifties for the pump, whereas I would likely be in my mid-sixties with the rod. I thought that in my late forties I would still be fit enough to have surgery, and if they had longer-lasting pump devices by then, I could upgrade. Alternatively, when the time came to have the pump replaced, I could swap it for the malleable rod, so that I didn't have to have any more surgeries. I did

not like the thought of having to go through surgeries in later life. Choosing the pump option, then, made the most logical sense to me.

With surgery approaching, I only had one concern: being able to look after myself. I was now single and a greater distance away from London. Two of my good friends, Ryan and Lucy, kindly offered me their spare room. They lived on the outskirts of Kent, so getting to St John & St Elizabeth Hospital would be straightforward from there. I am not very good at saying yes to help. I have had to learn a lot of humility in the process of lower surgery. Saying yes to my friends, for me, was a brave move. It proved to be a wise move too, the way things turned out. Perhaps this is a good reason never to say yes to a surgery date which falls on Friday the 13th.

Day of surgery – 13th January, 2017

Having stayed with Ryan and Lucy the night before, I headed to London in the morning. I was a bag of mixed emotions. Having settled back into life and enjoying being a single man, surgery was a mixed blessing. I was nervous to go through surgery recovery again but I was also excited to get the final stage over and done with and just get on with my life. I knew I had been lucky so far, having not had any complications. I worried this meant I might be due a complication with stage three. I tried to just stay realistic but optimistic.

Once I was settled into my gown and ready, a chap from Mr Bruno's surgical team visited, to go through the usual consent forms. He mentioned that if any problems with the urethra were found, the insertion of the erectile device would have to be abandoned. It is imperative that any issues with the urethra

are dealt with first. It is much harder to fix urethral issues once the device has been fitted. Of course, you just hope it won't happen to you, don't you?

Coming around from surgery, I vaguely remember someone talking to me. I thought it looked like Mr Bruno but I couldn't be sure – I could barely see, I was groggy and in and out of consciousness. All I remember is being told they had been unable to insert the erectile device, due to finding an issue in my urethra.

It was late by the time they got me settled back into my room. I gathered I wouldn't see anyone until the next day for an explanation of what had happened. I was disappointed, but of course I understood that these things occur. As upsetting as it was, I was okay.

Day 1 post-op

The night-time was okay, but the following day I was very upset. I was due for discharge at midday and I assumed one of the consultants would visit, explain what had happened and give me instructions for aftercare. However, nobody visited. A porter brought me my breakfast, but there was no sign of any nurses.

Eventually, a nurse came in, at around 10 am, and expressed surprise that I was still in bed. I explained that I hadn't been sure what to do. The nurse said she didn't know, left the room and didn't return. Later, another nurse appeared. I asked her if she knew any details about what had been done. What aftercare would I need? Was I still going home? I also explained that I was a little sore and hadn't had any pain relief since the night before. This nurse also disappeared and never returned. Finally, another nurse arrived to say that as they hadn't spoken with a consultant, I would have to stay another night. By this time,

it was way past midday. I resigned myself to another day in hospital, hoping for some clearer news later, and perhaps some attentive nurses.

However, no sooner had I given up for the day, then another nurse came in. She told me that she had spoken with Mr Bruno. She said that he was happy for me to leave. Shocked, I asked if I would be checked over before leaving, as no one had visited to look at my wounds. I also asked if the catheter needed to be removed before leaving.

She thought I didn't have a wound and also said the catheter would be removed in three weeks.

Having had a catheter before, I knew that in my case I could not leave the same urine bag on for three weeks or I would risk an infection. Also, I prefer to change to a bigger night bag when sleeping, so that I don't have to get up in the night to empty the bag. I also felt certain that despite not having had the device fitted, I had a wound. I could feel the bandage covering the area underneath my penis, and it was very sore too.

Trying to stay as calm as possible, I said, 'I'm sorry, I don't mean to be rude, but I am going to need spare catheter bags. I also need someone to have a look at these wounds before I leave, and let me know what aftercare I need.'

I was shaking now, and desperately trying to hold back tears of frustration.

'I just need to know what wounds I've got, and if I need to have sutures removed.'

The nurse had a quick look and announced, 'You have no wounds – it was done by keyhole.'

'Are you sure?' I protested. 'I'm really sore there and I can feel something...'

But she said she was sure and then left.

Biting my lip to hold back the tears, I struggled to get myself

up out of the bed. The catheter bag was full to the brim. I carefully detached it from the bed, carried it to the toilet with me, and emptied it out. Then I began to slowly take off my blood-stained net pants and peel the pads from underneath my penis. I intended to clean myself up as best I could before working out what to do next. I used my phone as a mirror, taking a picture so that I could see how things looked. There, as clear as day, was a 3-inch suture line under the base of my penis. They had opened up an area along the incision line of my vaginectomy. My frustration escalated to red-hot anger.

Taking deep breaths, I pulled on my hospital dressing gown. I headed out of my room and began to shuffle down the corridor towards the nurse's station. Seeing the nurse, as calmly as I could, I asked to speak to her. I explained that on washing myself I had found a wound.

The nurse still thought there couldn't be a wound.

I admit that I lost my temper then, thrusting my phone in her face and pointing to the picture I had taken. 'What the fuck do you call that then?' I shouted.

I am not proud of my reaction, but in my defence, by this point I was scared, confused and feeling incredibly vulnerable. In tears, I shuffled back to my room as quickly as I could.

Once back in my room, I called Ryan. Through snot-filled sobs, I told him all that was going on. The nurse arrived back in my room. She had rung Mr Bruno who confirmed to her that he'd told me everything I needed to know in theatre, so I could in fact go home. I was happy to be able to leave, but while I know surgeons do this, it isn't always easy to remember what they are telling you when you are still coming around from anaesthetic. Now I was clearer headed, I just needed someone to tell me the clear instructions I needed, and to explain why I had a wound if the device hadn't been fitted.

Within a couple of hours, both Ryan and Lucy arrived in my room. The nurse also returned and asked if I wanted dinner before I left. I didn't want food, I wanted to speak to the consultant, and to feel the staff knew what aftercare I needed. Ryan repeated my request. Could we have details of what wound care I needed, or any details whatsoever? The nurse said there were no notes, other than to say the device hadn't been fitted and I could be discharged. Having no other option, I was discharged without any clear instructions and we left.

Two days post-op

I spent the following day making calls and sending emails, trying to discover exactly what had been done to me during the procedure, and get some clear post-operative advice. By the end of the day I had not managed to gather much information at all. I was exhausted. After giving up in the early evening, I received a welcome message from Mr Bruno.

He told me what had been performed, though he didn't answer all my other questions. At the beginning of the surgery procedure, he tried to catheterize me and couldn't get the catheter tube through. On performing a cystoscopy (a camera into the bladder) to see what the problem was, he found 'a widening' in my urethra. He then abandoned the erectile device and repaired the urethra instead. This explained why I had a wound under my scrotum where he went in to fix the issue.

Mr Bruno informed me that although I was asymptomatic now, issues could arise later. It was best to get things fixed before fitting the erectile device. He went on to say that, once healed, I would be able to have the erectile device fitted. I was confused,

because surely a widening wouldn't prevent the catheter being inserted. I presumed he had got his words wrong and meant a narrowing – that the urethral pipe needed widening. I didn't email back to get it clarified. It was late in the day and I had just had enough of chasing my tail. I needed to put my energy into healing.

I really didn't feel well or right in myself, but I put it down to the traumatic experience. However, I had issues with the catheter immediately. My urine was various shades through pink to red. I emailed St Peter's to ask for advice and they replied that it was down to where I had been fixed and my urine would clear in time.

One week post-op

What then followed were endless, hellish days of catheter issues. I began passing blood clots and these kept blocking the catheter. In the early hours of the morning, just a few days post-surgery, Ryan had to drive me to the hospital because I risked going into urine retention. No urine was draining into my bag at all and I was bursting for a pee. Luckily, on the way, the tube cleared itself, and the urine drained through. The hospital checked me over, but really they couldn't do anything else, so they sent me away. Unfortunately, this issue kept repeating.

When I emailed Mr Stephens, he suggested that I have someone wash out my bladder. He suspected that there was likely a clot there that needed to be broken down and flushed through. None of the local medical centres was willing to do this. Unfortunately, because phalloplasty is so rarely seen in the community, a lot of clinics refuse to do anything. Eventually,

Mr Stephens told me to just come to see him and he would do it himself.

Two weeks post-op

At ten days post-op, off I went to London. As difficult as this journey was at such an early stage post-op, I was grateful for the chance to discuss things with Mr Stephens. I finally understood exactly what had been the issue that prevented fitting the erectile device. My urethral tube had developed what Mr Stephens called 'a cul-de-sac'. This meant that my urethra had a little outpouching near the base of my penis, like a false passageway. When they attempted to put the catheter tube through in surgery, it kept hitting this false passage. Although it hadn't been causing me issues, it likely would have done down the line. So, the decision had been to close that false passage, and abandon stage three, to allow my urethra to heal.

Mr Stephens also said that he suspected I had a bleed into my bladder during surgery, which is not uncommon. And a clot had formed, which was causing my bladder issues. However, he said he would try his best to clear it for me.

Having a bladder wash conjures images of a lovely soothing bath. Not the case at all. A bladder wash-out involves filling the bladder with water, holding it, and letting it drain. It is excruciatingly painful. It feels like your insides are going to explode. Mr Stephens was so kind and was full of apologies for causing me discomfort. He managed to get some clots out, but there were so many. He said it was likely that there were some exceptionally large pieces, and, because the catheter tube was so small, it would likely keep blocking. He said that the best course of action would be to take the catheter out early, in the hope

that any clots would then be more easily passed. He booked me into his clinic at the Spire in Slough for the following Saturday.

Catheter removal

Ryan very kindly offered to drive me to the Spire on the Saturday. After the catheter was removed, Mr Stephens told me to stay for a couple of hours, just to make sure I wasn't having any issues passing urine. I had no problem whatsoever; in fact, I couldn't stop peeing. I attributed this to the amount of water I had drunk and thought it would improve. It didn't. Driving back from the Spire to Kent, the urge to pee was excruciating. Poor Ryan kept having to stop to find me somewhere to go. But no sooner than I went, as soon as we headed off again, the urge to pee would return. I tried to fight it, but it was no use – my bladder just would not respond to logic. Once we hit the motorway, I was out of options. I was sweating and my heart was racing, I was jigging up and down in the passenger seat, desperately trying to overrule my bladder. Embarrassingly, I had to just get a bottle in the end and try to pee in that, as Ryan drove the rest of the way back to his home.

The urges did not let up. In the days that followed, my urine was still alternating between shades of pink to red. I had such extreme urgency to use the toilet. I was going to the toilet about every 15 minutes, both day and night. It was hugely distressing as well as painful to urinate, and of course it meant I wasn't getting any sleep. Mr Stephens reassured me that it was likely due to the clots in my bladder causing irritation. He said that the antibiotics I was on would kill any potential infection.

By now, I had stayed with Lucy and Ryan for far longer than I had intended. I was hugely grateful, and they were more than

happy to have me stay, but I needed to get home and continue to heal in my own surroundings.

Travelling home was going to be a challenge with the frequent urination issue. It would be a five-hour journey from Kent to Devon. The only way I could do it was by wearing an adult nappy. This was my only option. I had had too many close calls by now. Once the urge to pee became strong, trying to hold it was impossible. So, I ordered myself some maximum-protection incontinence pants. This was the only way I could ensure making it home with my dignity intact (at least, as dignifying as peeing into an adult diaper, whilst sat on a National Express coach, could be).

One month post-op

Reaching a month post-op, the peeing urges continued. Since arriving home, I'd had two more hellish weeks of not being able to go more than about 20 minutes without having to pee. I was sleep-deprived and stressed, and my mental health was declining rapidly.

The hardest thing to deal with was that the pain and distress felt like they had no purpose. With stages one and two, I had managed the pain and frustration because they had a positive outcome. In stage one, the pain and frustration meant I gained a penis. In stage two, the pain and frustration meant I gained the ability to stand to pee. In this stage of surgery, I had gained nothing.

I tried to reason with myself. I reminded myself that at least the issue had been found. At least it had been fixed now rather than further down the line. I tried so hard to see that as the reason for this surgery. But it was just so hard to lift myself up.

My post-op experience had caused me additional stress. I am very aware of how mental states can affect physical wellbeing, and I think that experience did affect my healing.

As the bladder issues were not improving, I contacted St Peter's again. I felt they must be sick of me by now. However, as I was rapidly learning, it was vital that I advocated strongly for myself. With aftercare sometimes sketchy, making sure to get the right information, so we can look after ourselves as best as possible, is vital. Mr Stephens ordered another urine test, and another course of antibiotics, as well as oxybutynin medication for bladder frequency. The oxybutynin helped a little, allowing me roughly an hour between toilet visits. However, the painful burning on urination remained. The urine test came back showing infection. The antibiotic I was taking should have solved it; however, the doctor found it necessary to prescribe a second course. A repeat urine test came back infection-free, but I still had burning and frequency. By now, approaching six weeks post-op, it was apparent that these issues were not due to infection but something else. Therefore, the decision was made to admit me to hospital for a cystoscopy, where they would insert a tiny camera into my bladder, to investigate these issues further.

Cystoscopy procedure – 3rd March, 2017

Soon after, I received a date for the cystoscopy. This procedure would be at the Highgate Private Hospital, under the care of Mr Bruno. I would rather it had been with Mr Stephens, but at least this time I knew not to expect good post-op communication, and I could be more prepared for that. Not an ideal situation really – I think effective communication after a surgical procedure is

vital. However, I knew I could email Mr Stephens afterwards if I needed to. He always answered and was always incredibly helpful. Most importantly, I was relieved this procedure was in a different hospital. After all, it had been the issues with the aftercare which had had the worst effect on me after the previous surgery.

When I woke after the cystoscopy surgery, like the previous time, Mr Bruno leant over me and began to explain what he had done. I can understand a surgeon wanting to tell a patient straight away, and I'm sure some patients are keen to hear how things have gone as soon as possible, but I doubt many people can really take in information when under the influence of anaesthetic. All I remember is him mentioning the word 'unhooking'.

Later, once I was back in my room and had come around a bit, I had a look under the covers. I could see that a catheter was coming out from underneath my penis, just behind the scrotum. Nothing was attached to my penis at all. My heart sank like a stone. I realized that I had in fact been unhooked and would now be sitting down to pee.

I felt utterly devastated and shocked. When a nurse appeared, I asked if I could see Mr Bruno. I had been willing to let his poor communication slide. However, considering the unhooking, I needed to know why he had felt it necessary to take such drastic measures. I hadn't anticipated that this might happen to me. Given how devastating a backwards step such as this can be, I'd really hoped to be able to discuss it with the surgeon. The nurses this time were completely different to my previous experience. A very kind nurse, on seeing how distraught I was, managed to get Mr Bruno to visit me.

When he appeared in my room, Mr Bruno explained that I had a 'narrowing' in my urethra. He told me that he had fixed it,

and in order for it to heal, he had made a hole for me to urinate through, just under my scrotum. I would have the catheter in for two weeks while my urethra healed. And as long as I had no issues after the catheter was removed, I could have surgery in a couple of months to reconnect the urethra.

I was fuming, but not just because of the decision to unhook me. As upsetting as it was, I knew that it happened sometimes. I had seen this occur with other guys when the urethra was damaged. Unhooking allows the surgically created urethra to properly heal before being hooked back up. I understood the logic in this. I understood how delicate and difficult the urethral part of our surgery is. I also knew how important it was that any issues were resolved before fitting the erectile device. However, what I wanted to know was what was wrong with my urethra that led him to make this decision? What had caused the burning and frequency of urination? It was just so hard for me to accept all of this without a fuller explanation. To go from a straightforward issue-free urethral hook-up and peeing normally, to being unhooked, was utterly devastating.

One week post-op

After I was discharged from hospital I went to stay with Ryan and Lucy again. This time my physical recovery was far less eventful. My urine was clear and free from clots. Apart from the new surgical site, I was pain-free. My bladder was now acting normally. With a catheter fitted, I was at last finally sleeping through the entire night.

Emotionally, though, I was in a state. The whole experience had been very traumatic for me and had taken its toll on me. The post-op experience, including what I felt was a lack of clear

instructions and information, had all caused so much stress and anger, and this left a bitter sting.

Then, of course, there was the issue of the backwards step. Standing to pee had solved so much of my dysphoria. Having this ability taken away, no matter how temporarily, was a huge blow. I felt as if I had fallen so far backwards. I didn't just need one surgery now; I needed at least two. First, I would have to have my urethra hooked back up, and only when it was okay could I be relisted for stage three. Making this worse was the way that the new hole for weeing had been created under my penis. It was not just a hole, it was more of a slit. In many ways, it looked like my old vagina. I knew logically that it wasn't, but that was how it looked. My dysphoria was once again screaming at me.

My dear friends very wisely advised that I let it go as best I could. I needed to save my energy and focus on recovering from the two surgeries. One's state of mind has a direct effect on healing, and I knew I wouldn't heal well if I didn't just let the anger go. I was better off using my energy to deal with this massive emotional blow. I needed to accept the backwards step and the finish line being moved forward indefinitely. It would take some time to get myself back on an even keel mentally and emotionally.

Two weeks post-op

On returning home to Dawlish, I remained issue-free and my catheter was removed. The pain on peeing didn't return and neither did the bladder urgency. Over a few weeks, my bladder tone returned and I was able to hold my urine without fear of an accident. This was a relief in every sense of the word.

Mentally, though, I was struggling to heal from the experience.

I was reliving the hospital experience and dreaming about it. Then there was the re-emergence of dysphoria as I returned to sit to pee. Every time I sat on the toilet, every time I wiped underneath my penis, a little bit more of me crumbled inside.

I had a follow-up appointment on the 10th May with Mr Stephens. He examined me, which I have to say was done with much care and respect. Having my legs open and Mr Stephens examining where the new slit was, brought back awful memories of smear tests. I lay on that couch, not knowing whether to vomit or sob.

We discussed rehooking my urethra. When this had first been discussed, it was assumed I would need a mucosal mouth graft. This is where they take a small bit of skin from the lining of your cheeks to repair the urethra. Often, the rehooking of the urethra needs to be done in two stages. The first stage is to create a new piece of urethra from the mouth graft, which is then allowed time to heal. Then, once healed, a second surgery connects the new urethra with the old urethra. However, after examining me, Mr Stephens said it looked like I had enough good skin down there to rehook me without using a mouth graft. This meant that it could be done in one stage rather than two separate stages. He said he was 90 per cent sure this would be the case. The worst-case scenario, he said, was that he might need to take a small piece of skin from my mouth but likely not a full graft. This was at least some relief. He estimated it could be done around June or July. The trouble was, that would be right when I would be having exams. I knew, however, that surgeons' estimated dates for surgery are very different from the reality. Therefore, I just agreed to being relisted for rehooking and would deal with the date when it came up. I braced myself to cope with many more uncomfortable, dysphoria-filled months.

An Unexpected Sexual Awakening

Recovering from the failed stage three attempt took time. I needed space to heal from the trauma of the two surgeries. I also had to find a way to make temporary peace with the way my genitals had been reconfigured. Additionally, I needed to change the plans I had made. I had been looking ahead to 2017 being the year I completed my surgery, so that I could be free to just get on with my life. One of my plans had been to start looking at dating opportunities. However, I had not wanted to start dating before completing my surgery, so any dating plans were back on hold.

I'd been single for a year by this point and I had greatly valued that time. I had never been single for an extended period before. My mental health issues had made me very codependent in earlier relationships. I had rarely been without a partner for more than a month or two. I was determined to make sure that the next time I began a relationship, it would be a healthy, interdependent one. I was therefore in no rush to end my single life, but I was excited to begin dating again and to have my first sexual experience as a penis owner.

The other reason I had been keen to start dating was that I had some exploring to do. After splitting up with Alex, I found myself confused about whom I should date. I had imagined that I would be a straight man in my new single life, returning to dating women. I thought I had only been able to love Alex as a man because I was already in a relationship with him. However, during the year I had been single, I noticed a growing attraction to men. More significantly, there didn't seem to be any women who interested me at all. I felt baffled by my attraction to men but also keen to explore this feeling, if a little anxious.

But, with the failure of the final stage of surgery, and the new uncertainty of when surgery would be finished, I had shelved all my plans for dating. There was little I could do about working out my attraction because I was in the middle of surgery. I didn't want to date anyone until it was complete. I was of the mindset that the next stage of my life, exploring my sexuality, would happen after my phalloplasty was finished. Besides, the way I'd been reopened underneath meant that my dysphoria was too intense to even consider having an intimate relationship. I pushed the questioning out of my mind, telling myself I would deal with it later. However, life had a very different plan for me.

Before the surgery setback, I had been looking for ways to work through my sexuality issues without having to date. I'd been reading about exploring intimacy through cuddle party workshops. Cuddle parties were a kind of therapy, helping people to explore boundaries with guided consensual touch. As terrifying as the concept sounded, I was also intrigued to see whether it might help me. A friend of mine knew someone who worked in a similar therapeutic field and kindly put me in touch with a woman called Erin, a Sexological Bodyworker. Broadly speaking, this meant that she worked therapeutically to

help people connect with their bodies and with their sexuality. We chatted online and she put my mind at ease about the cuddle workshop and encouraged me to try it. By a peculiar twist of fate, she was due to visit Dawlish to attend a workshop and we agreed to meet up. There was no hint of anything other than a friendly meeting.

On meeting, Erin and I chatted easily and laughed together. It was impossible not to like her. At the time, I didn't notice any attraction to her, other than on a friendship level. Reflecting on our initial meeting, I believe the reason I didn't notice any attraction was because my body and heart were in self-protect mode. I was still traumatized and recovering from the surgical process. I couldn't imagine being intimate with anyone in the poor mental and physical state I was in.

However, in the weeks that followed, Erin and I continued to message one another. The flirting began to escalate. On realizing I was starting to have feelings for her, I panicked. Not feeling at all ready for anything, I tried to cut things off. If it had been anyone else, I am sure they would have just given up and run a mile. However, Erin was experienced at interacting with people who'd experienced trauma. She could see that I was very vulnerable and torn between my head and my heart. Erin was therefore persistent, but in a very gentle and understanding way. It was precisely because of her tenderness and respect for what I was going through that I eventually agreed to travel to her hometown of Bath to visit her, despite my fears.

Arriving late on the Friday evening, Erin picked me up from Bath station. Once again, we were at ease in each other's company. But, this time, there was a tension in the air. It was clear things were on the cusp of changing from a friendship to something more.

Erin's experiences as a Sexological Bodyworker meant she

was comfortable and confident in talking openly about how she felt about me. I, however, wasn't. I seemed to have regressed to being a teenager, and one that had no idea how to voice their feelings. The most I could manage was to nod in agreement that I did feel attracted to her.

Erin was kind and patient as the weekend progressed. We cuddled and Erin made it clear she wanted more if I wanted that too. But I was frozen with fear and couldn't find the courage to act. I couldn't get out of my head enough to connect with any feelings. It was only because of Erin's kindness and skills with dealing with people like me, who had intimacy issues, that I didn't run. I desperately wanted to relax enough to try to be intimate, so I trusted her, and we just kept taking tiny steps.

By Monday night we still hadn't advanced past the cuddling stage. I was getting annoyed with myself and concerned. What if it wasn't nerves and I just didn't feel anything? Why couldn't I tell? I knew something was there. I had an awareness of a feeling but was unable to connect with that feeling. I was sleeping in Erin's spare room and as I was climbing into bed that night, Erin popped in to say goodnight.

'Can I kiss you?' she asked gently.

Swallowing a fireball of nerves, I nodded yes. As our lips met, I felt a stiffening, but not where I wanted to feel it. My whole body stiffened up like there was a solid wall between me and Erin, but also a solid wall between me and my internal feelings. What on earth was going on with me? We said goodnight and Erin went to her own room. I was left staring up at the ceiling, my mind a tornado of thoughts.

The next morning, I sheepishly walked into Erin's kitchen. I felt painfully awkward and entirely unable to communicate how I felt. One part of me was wishing the time away until I could leave; wanting to run from these confusing feelings. The other

part of me was desperate to run towards what was happening; wanting to push against the barrier between me and the feelings that I intuitively knew were there but couldn't physically feel.

We spent the day together out shopping and walking around the town. This helped me to relax and we became increasingly more intimate as the day progressed. That afternoon, we came back and lay on Erin's bed. There had been no intention other than to just cuddle and relax before heading off to dinner with our mutual friends that evening.

'Can I put my hand on your cock?' Erin asked softly. 'Just on the outside of your jeans?'

It was a good job I was lying down, otherwise I'd likely have fainted. This request from anyone else but Erin would have shocked me into a full-blown pack-my-bags-and-run scenario. However, this was the kind of touch that Erin performed as a Sexological Bodyworker – touch that had strict boundaries and consent. Therefore, I felt safe that Erin would only do what I agreed to and no more.

I took a deep breath and said yes. As Erin laid her hand gently on my cock, a rush of feelings overcame me like water bursting from a dam. I felt myself get hard beneath her hand. My entire groin began to throb in a way I had never felt before. The pulsating and burning between my legs was intense to the point of being painful.

The rush of emotion was a powerful tidal wave. With that rush came the relief that I wasn't emotionally dead. All the fear melted away and I gave myself completely to Erin. Watching and feeling her explore my cock was not only erotic but emotive too. To see and feel my cock in someone else's hands was both surreal and intensely emotional. To see my body being held and touched in a way that was congruent with my gender was overwhelmingly self-affirming.

Erin intuitively seemed to know to be gently inquisitive, and careful. She was aware of my issues with being opened underneath my penis and respectfully avoided that area. Feeling her hand close around my cock and gently stroke me left me on fire and I could not contain my pleasure.

When Erin began to explore me with her tongue, and I watched and felt her slide my cock into her mouth, I thought my whole body was going to spontaneously combust. For the first time in my life, I felt like a man sexually. With that new awareness of myself, I felt much of the lower dysphoria melt away. It didn't matter that my cock wasn't hard – it wasn't an issue. We moved together and when I came, I felt a lifetime of tension surge through my body and burn as it left me.

I couldn't believe I could feel this comfortable sexually, despite my incomplete surgery. Regardless of having a soft penis and parts which shouldn't be there, I didn't feel incomplete. Neither did I feel inadequate or inept, as I expected to feel. I didn't need a completed surgery to feel male. Regardless of the state of my genitals, I felt empowered and my gender felt affirmed.

I knew my first time having sex would be special but I did not expect it to come midway through surgery. This was my first time having sex as me, the true male me, and I didn't even need a fully working penis to experience it. The impact was profound. With this experience, it was as if a missing piece of my gender jigsaw slotted into place, and I don't mean the obvious. I hadn't realized until that moment that I hadn't moved into my male sexuality.

To explain, I had made the transition to live as a male socially, mentally and physically. Those key areas were well developed, having lived as Finn for five years by this point. However, I hadn't moved into my maleness in a sexual sense. I was still carrying the weight of my earlier sexual experiences living as a female,

which had been anything but good. I had no idea what it was like to have sex as a man, with this new male body of mine.

This awakening also made me realize how much I had been repressing my sexual feelings. My sex drive, which although still higher than it had been pre-testosterone, had lessened so much since the early days. After the first experience with Erin, my sex drive returned to peak levels. Making sense of this, it was likely that when my sex drive first peaked, I didn't have the outlet to explore it. This wasn't Alex's fault by any means. I'd entered the relationship with lots of sexual issues which I'd carried for years. Then, of course, by the time my sex drive arrived, Alex and I were already in a pattern of not having sex. I felt ashamed for my constant wanking and so I must have subconsciously shut my sex drive back down. In one glorious moment of intimacy, Erin had managed to undo years of sexual trauma. She had awakened a new sexual connection between my body and my mind, which would forever change things for me. I knew now that I need not put things off until after I completed surgery. With the right person, my differently configured body didn't matter. Suddenly, a whole new world opened up to me and with it an enthusiasm for new adventures.

It wasn't just the sexual experience which changed me, but also the things I learned from Erin about relationships. Erin was polyamorous, which meant she was open to having multiple partners of varying intimate connections. When Erin had first told me that she was poly, I was gutted. I couldn't imagine having more than one partner and not feeling jealous. Therefore, I had thought it very unlikely that Erin and I would have a relationship. However, after a lot of reflection, I found that it wasn't the deal-breaker I had initially thought it to be. More importantly, I could see how polyamory could make perfect sense in my situation.

Being intimate with Erin had shown me that I still had an attraction to females. However, my attraction to men was still there too. Now that my sexuality had been awakened, so had my desire to explore my attraction to men. I hadn't known how to begin to explore this. One-night stands were not my thing. Being in recovery, I didn't go to bars and meet people. I could join a dating app and then go on various dates with people of different genders. However, I didn't like the sound of that either because I could hurt people, and that did not sit right with my moral compass. The remarkable thing about polyamory was that it would allow me to see different people but in a way that was consensual with both parties. This would provide a much healthier basis for sexual exploration, one where there was lots of communication and trust-building. Trust would play a vital part in any exploration, otherwise I risked undoing the healing work I had done so far. Any intimacy I had, I wanted it to be from the basis of kindness and compassion from both parties, which was something I wouldn't be able to achieve with one-night stands. I couldn't believe I was thinking this, but it did make complete sense for what I needed at the time.

Keen to explore this idea and look for potential dates, I began to connect with people online who were also polyamorous. I turned to my LGBT community first, as I felt more comfortable there. It turned out that I had many friends who practised a degree of polyamory. I was taken aback by this being such a new concept to me but old news to many in my community. Perhaps, as LGBT people, we are more open to doing things differently and having an open mind.

After posting online about my discovery of polyamory, a friend whom I knew briefly through my YouTube channel messaged me. Owen, a transgender male, was in a polyamorous relationship with Frankie, a non-binary person, assigned female

at birth. They were an established couple but occasionally saw other people. I joked with them about my being their play partner but I wasn't really joking at all. Owen took my hint. He said that he and Frankie had considered experimenting with a third person in their relationship. After we had chatted for a while, they invited me to visit them and to see what developed.

Spurred on by my newly found sexual confidence, thanks to Erin, I found the courage to say yes. As terrified as I was at the thought of two people, I also thought that it might in many ways be safer. There would be less chance of getting emotionally attached. This would be a negotiated consensual hook-up, for want of a better word, with no strings attached. It was also a chance to experience being with another man, which I was by now desperate to try.

Off I went then, on another adventure, this time full of open-minded enthusiasm. On the journey across to Cardiff, I was struck by how different my journey to Bath had been, just a few short weeks earlier. It was incredible to notice how connected to my body I felt and how sexually awake I was. More surprising than anything, though, was my level of courage. As I reflected on how much I had changed and grown, my eyes welled with tears of gratitude for Erin.

Owen met me at the coach station. It wasn't awkward at all. We had chatted enough online over the years to feel instantly comfortable. We took a walk back to the home he shared with Frankie and waited for them to arrive home from work. Later that evening, the three of us moved from chatting lightly about ourselves to talking directly about sex. I bravely said that I was willing and incredibly happy to experiment with them. I felt attracted to them both and felt able to trust them. This led to an enormously exciting few days of hanging out together as a thrupple. We even ventured out around Cardiff, all three of us

holding hands. The novelty of it added to the thrill. I was aching to get naked with them both.

On our second evening together, the three of us cuddled up on the sofa, watching TV. Tentatively, the cuddling became kissing and gentle touching, testing out how it felt. Then finally, we moved to the bedroom and began to undress one another. Having sex as a group of three people, is absolutely nothing like the threesomes you see on porn sites. This was such a beautiful sharing of space and bodies. All three of us understood that trans people's bodies can be problematic when it comes to intimacy, therefore there was lots of checking in with each other and being mindful of each other's needs. There was no awkwardness, just lots of sharing each other and pleasuring each other. Owen had not had lower surgery but he wore a prosthetic penis. This was the thing I had been the most excited about in my new exploration: the chance to have anal sex with another man.

Before I had lower surgery, anal sex did not cross my mind. In fact, if it had been suggested to me, I'd have run a mile. It was after stage two that I began to find anal sex arousing and pleasurable. I have often wondered why my thoughts about anal sex changed. Perhaps in no longer having my vagina, I craved penetration in another way.

I was never entirely keen on vaginal penetration, though. Before transition, when dating men, vaginal penetration was something which I only enjoyed briefly, when highly aroused. When dating women, I enjoyed penetration far more, as long as it was only with fingers. Once I realized that I was transgender, though, penetration caused too much dysphoria. I moved to preferring the focus to be on my T-dick, and on the outskirts of my Batcave, so to speak. The sudden desire for anal penetration, then, was rather a surprise. It was an even greater surprise when I realized how much I enjoyed it.

I have chatted with other trans guys who discovered a love of anal sex post-surgery. I wonder if our G-spots shift position as a result of vaginectomy. Or perhaps things are changed in some other way which makes anal sex feel so much more pleasurable. Whatever the cause, anal penetration had become my favourite part of solo masturbation. I had only ever used an anal dildo and only on my own. I was incredibly keen to experience being a bottom for another man.

As excited as I was to have anal sex, I was also nervous. Enjoying a dildo up my ass on my own was one thing. Having someone else involved was quite another. There was the worry of cleanliness. On my own, if a bit of poop appeared, I could deal with that. Having a bit of poop appear in the company of someone else, however... That would be mortifying. As a complete novice to being a bottom, I had no idea if I would feel the same way about anal penetration when someone else was doing it.

My new confidence, keenness and sky-high sex drive thrust me through the fear and onto all fours. Having Owen inside me felt magnificent. I had no idea that sex could feel that good. The last thing I was concerned about, as I pushed back hard against Owen's groin, was the presence of any poop. Frankie now had my cock in their mouth and Owen, spurred on by my eager pushing backwards, moved from slowly sliding in and out of me into thrusting into me. Owen's thighs slapped against my arse cheeks, as I came harder than I had ever come in my life.

Just like the experience with Erin, my time with Owen and Frankie had deeper meaning than the bodily connection. Being naked with two other trans people had brought even more gender affirmation. To be intimate with two trans bodies of different configurations helped me to see that gender is not dependent on body presentation. Of course, I knew this already, but there is a difference between knowing and experiencing. It

was noticing my own reaction to Owen's and Frankie's bodies which helped me to see this truth. If I could see someone's differently presented body yet still see them as the gender they are, then of course other people could have the same experience seeing my naked body.

During all this excitement, Finn Jr. celebrated his second birthday, and he was certainly having quite the celebration. Looking at the progress I had made was astounding. My body was in great shape, having healed well, even from the most recent surgery.

Being intimate with people had increased my body confidence significantly. I didn't have a perfect body according to conventional standards – I was heavily scarred from all the surgeries and carrying a bit more belly than I'd have liked – but it was my perfect body. My scars had healed well, though. Areas I'd had concerns about, such as the glans of my penis with its self-harm scars circling the tip, had stopped bothering me. Having someone else explore Finn Jr. with the same love and curiosity that I felt for him had shown me how perfect he was, even with scars.

I'd also been a bit anxious about my bum scars, especially with how purple and wide they still were. They had lightened a bit but were still very visible. I also had small dog ears on the side of my hip at the end of the stitch line. Walking around naked in front of Erin, Owen and Frankie soon helped me to let go of those worries too. Erin had recommended trying castor oil on those scars. I'd only been using it for a couple of months by this point but there was a noticeable difference.

My arm was the most astounding piece of healing to witness. I had been extremely lucky to have a graft that took so well. The scar was still prominent, but it always would be, to some extent. Again, being intimate with others highlighted that these scars

did not matter one bit. I was, of course, still treating my scars with care, massaging them morning and night with tamanu oil. I was still seeing some darker pigmentation on the graft, despite covering it with sunblock and tattoo sleeves when outside. I had read that grafts could often produce more pigmentation in the healing process and that it might settle with time. It's funny really, considering that skin came from under my bum, which had never seen the light of day before.

Of course, it was Finn Jr. himself who had the most significant leap forward in healing, especially in regaining sensation. Until my first sexual experience with Erin, I thought my sensation hadn't changed much. However, in being intimate I discovered that I had much more feeling than I realized. Importantly, during my summer of exploration, the sensation appeared to have increased even further.

Perhaps this was because it was someone else touching my penis and therefore I noticed sensation differently. Perhaps touching and sex had stimulated the nerves further, thus increasing sensation. It could also have been a mental thing, being my first time having sex as a man. This may have just brought me into a greater awareness of my genitals and the feeling there. I know that it also really helped to have my body treated as an object of love and lust for a change, rather than a medical site. More likely, it was all these things which contributed to my awareness and increase of sensation.

The most surprising development for me at this point was the sudden decrease in dysphoria. This was even more surprising, considering that just a few months earlier I'd had the largest increase in dysphoria on being opened underneath my penis. Reflecting on this, I think the decrease in dysphoria was partly for the same reason as the increase in sensation. I had moved into a new comfortableness in my body and a greater sense of

assuredness in my masculinity. Experiencing pleasure in the hands of another had helped me to see that, finished or unfinished, I was still male, I was whole, I was enough.

The other cause for the decrease in dysphoria was most certainly Erin. She had skilfully and gently steered me into relaxing enough to allow her to touch the parts I feared the most. In slow increments I even began to allow her to touch the opened-up part underneath my penis. Surprisingly, I even managed to find pleasure in that area. As I allowed Erin to touch more and more of me, my sexual barriers melted. This relaxing opened an entirely new sexual feeling where I could feel arousal in every part of my body.

It became clear that the dysphoria had been causing numerous mental blocks. Understandably, dysphoria had previously made it impossible to be aroused without also feeling anxious. This meant I had, in many ways, compartmentalized my genitals. I had strict boundaries of which areas were okay and which areas weren't. This survival tactic was limiting my enjoyment of my body by fragmenting my genitals into several separate parts. I had unconsciously separated my body into fragments of old parts, new parts, male parts, female parts. Realizing this, I also realized the truth: there were no parts. It was all my penis. Yes, my penis was constantly changing through surgery, but it was still one entity and none of it was female.

Erin had shown me that it was safe to step towards the dysphoria rather than step away from it. In doing so, I was free to enjoy every part of me. With this new awareness, suddenly everything felt male, even the open underneath area. I could now see that setting strict rules, for myself and others in how to touch my body, was limiting my capacity to feel the full spectrum of sexual feeling.

The new awareness of my genitals and the new way of seeing

them made me re-evaluate the words I used for them. In the early days of transition, the term 'T-dick' had helped me to deal with the dysphoria around the word 'clitoris'. Moving to call the clitoris my T-dick was of major help in affirming my maleness. But, considering the way sensation had changed, and considering my recent sexual experiences, this term suddenly felt incorrect. It separated my parts into old and new and this and that. My newly reconfigured clitoris was part of my new penis; it wasn't separate, so I renamed this area my 'base dick'.

This symbolic joining of parts also made sense with how reaching orgasm was also changing. The area where the clitoris had been buried was still a significant arousal site. However, the arousal there was now more incorporated with the rest of my penis. My clitoris still got erect, and when it did, the arousal sensation took over my whole groin. In many ways, now that I was feeling the entire area, the erection made it feel like my penis got hard too.

To reach orgasm, I still needed to stimulate my base dick, but not in the way I once had. I could now stimulate that area more indirectly. When stroking my penis during masturbation, the action of pulling my penis also pulled and stimulated my base dick. And the back-and-forth action of my hand, hitting on my base dick, stimulated me too. So, although still relying on my old buried equipment to orgasm, it was more in an indirect way. This further added to my buried clitoris not feeling like something separate any more, but part of my new penis itself.

I started to think differently about sensation at this point too. As sensation had gradually appeared, it had not been in the way I imagined at all. The sensation was still largely displaced. For example, on touching my penis, I would feel the touch in my base dick, not in my newly created penis. I had been waiting to feel the sensation directly on my penis. However, it suddenly dawned

on me that what I was feeling was still sensation, regardless of where I actually felt it. At this point, I felt all erotic sensation, no matter where I was touched on my penis, in my base dick. But I was also beginning to notice that I could feel some direct touch, but that was tactile sensation rather than erotic. Regardless, it was clear I was gaining increasing amounts of both tactile and erotic sensation – just not in the way I initially imagined.

It's funny because when I decided to draft this book, it was not in my plan to talk about sex at all. Now, in hindsight, and considering my earth-shattering sexual awakening, that intention seems daft. I mean, having a penis created, you would think automatically that sex comes to mind, wouldn't you? My sexual adventure made me realize just how asleep I had been sexually. I think having been through so many surgeries, my penis felt medicalized in ways that I hadn't realized. This meant that coupled with my poor past experiences around sex, my body dysphoria and then medicalization, it's no wonder I was shut off sexually.

I could see parallels in my sexual awakening with my first few months of getting sober. I had numbed myself for years with alcohol and drugs as feeling was too painful. In sobriety, I suddenly got my feelings back and I had no emotional dictionary to describe them. I instead had to learn from scratch to name my emotions and manage them. In the same way, I had no sexual dictionary. I had never had a healthy sex life. My body had been a source of pain and I had switched off from it. Now, I needed to learn what I was feeling, what I liked, and so on. I found myself in awe at the limitless kaleidoscope of emotions and sensations that I'd had no idea I was capable of feeling.

The new awareness also made my sexuality confusion make a lot more sense. I think you need to deeply know and own your gender identity before you can truly know who you are attracted

to. How can you possibly feel attracted sexually to anyone if you don't first know who you are in relation to that other person?

The experiences I had with Erin, and with Owen and Frankie, were instrumental in a dramatic decrease in dysphoria. These experiences were also a key part in overcoming the trauma of the failed stage three surgeries, and in healing my mental health. I could see now that they would also be key going forward in exploring my sexuality further. I was in an amazing place, feeling more confident and happier than I had in many years. So much so, that when I got the call for surgery, despite wanting my urethra rehooked, I was loath to call a halt to my summer of sexual exploration.

Peeing Freely Again

Rehook-Up Success

The call for surgery wasn't just an unwelcome interruption of my exciting sexual summer. It also came at a particularly challenging time. Earlier in the year, my mum had become ill. Mum being poorly wasn't anything new. However, it was clear that, this time, her health was not likely to recover. It looked as if she had developed dementia, which later on was confirmed. A chest infection, lack of oxygen and damage from many strokes over the years had caused a brain event. What resulted was a rapidly advancing vascular dementia. I decided that, as Mum had little time left, I would move from Devon back to my home-town of Eastbourne. Mum had supported me in my transition and accepted me as her son. I could think of no greater way to thank her than to look after her in her time of need.

In late September, 2017, St Peter's called and offered me a date for rehook-up on the 2nd October. At the time, I was still living between two homes: my flat in Devon and Mum's flat in Eastbourne. Having surgery in the middle of all this would be a challenge. However, I decided that I just wanted it done. With any luck, the rehook-up would be straightforward. Either way,

the recovery wouldn't be as intense as either stage one or stage two. I felt confident that I could manage.

That's not to say I wasn't worried about the surgery. I had huge fears that they might find my urethra was so damaged that a rehook-up wouldn't work; or that the surgery might go wrong, and I'd have to be unhooked again. The thought of never being able to stand to pee was a terrifying one. Although I had made huge progress with the management of my gender dysphoria, I still held on to the hope that one day I'd be peeing problem-free again. If that didn't happen, I would have to find a way to live with that. I didn't want to think about it, but at the same time I knew I had to manage my expectations so as not to be let down.

I also had some concerns that the surgery would take place at St John & St Elizabeth Hospital again. After my previous traumatic experience, I was fearful to return. I couldn't help but associate it to a really awful time in my surgery journey.

On the morning of the surgery, I made my way to London. Owen kindly offered to come with me and I gratefully accepted. I was glad of the company and support. Arriving at the hospital, I was shown to my room and began to unpack. Before long, a young nurse with a warm smile came to explain all the pre-op checks that were to be done. By now I was an expert and I knew the drill with my eyes closed. The nurse left me to do my MRSA swabs. It's much nicer not to have a nurse watch you when you are sticking a cotton wool swab up your arse.

Mr Stephens soon appeared. He ran through what we'd talked about at our last appointment. He reminded me that, if he could, he would repair the urethra with some skin from the open area under my penis. If he couldn't use that skin, he would take a graft from inside my mouth. Again, he reminded me that he was 80–90 per cent sure that I wouldn't need a graft, but he wanted

me to be prepared just in case. We chatted for a few moments, and he mentioned he had seen some of my YouTube videos. I cringed at that. It's always strange for me when professionals tell me they've watched them. As he was heading out the room, he stopped abruptly, grinned and said, 'Don't worry, I will come to see you after.'

Soon afterwards, a nurse came to collect me and walked me across to theatre. By now I was used to the walk and used it as valuable time to take some deep breaths and set my intentions to deal with whatever I woke up with.

It is always strange waking up from anaesthetic and feeling like you only passed out seconds ago. As my vision cleared, Mr Stephens's smiling face came into focus. 'It's all gone to plan,' he told me, through a wide grin.

I'd only been in theatre for about an hour and 45 minutes and apparently everything had been very straightforward. On being wheeled back to my room, I was surprised and happy to see Owen still there. To have someone to share the joy that the rehook-up had been straightforward was wonderful. I was feeling comfortable and the pain was minimal. Owen stayed with me for a while until the grogginess overpowered my excitedness and I nodded off.

The care this time was remarkably different. During the night, the nurses that checked on me were attentive and promptly brought me pain relief for what remained only mild pain. I didn't see any of the nurses from my previous stay. Someone suggested they could have been bank nurses. My last surgery was on a public holiday, so that's possible. To be honest, though, many trans people have horror stories about their care. It isn't just me and there doesn't seem to be a pattern to these bad experiences, in that they weren't tied to a particular hospital.

This leads me to think that the problem may well be individual nurses, rather than a hospital team. Unfortunately, there is still a lot of bad feeling towards trans people and with that comes a lot of discrimination. I would like to think that people in the caring profession would be immune to prejudice, but they are human and so are not. Fortunately, over my entire transition I have had far many more positive experiences with nurses than negative ones. Most nurses have gone out of their way to be supportive and kind, and I am eternally grateful for their compassion and care.

The following morning, I awoke feeling well rested and with minimal pain. A nurse visited to help me wash and dress. As all had gone well, I would be discharged at midday. Mr Stephens came again to check things over and he repeated how straightforward the surgery had been and how happy he was. We talked about the catheter and he suggested that, rather than draining into a bag, I might try a flip-flow valve. This would allow my bladder to work as normally as possible and might eliminate the usual issues I had with catheters. I agreed, although I asked to have a catheter bag for the way home. Travelling on public transport, I couldn't guarantee I'd be able to find a toilet easily and I didn't want to stress me or my bladder.

I had decided to make my own way home. The journey was straightforward to Eastbourne. Taxi to the station, one train home, then taxi to Mum's, where I was staying. Not ideal – and if the surgery had been more complicated, I would have asked a friend to ferry me – but as things were, it was manageable. Recovery from this surgery was going to be a bit of a challenge with my mum so ill. Ryan and Lucy had offered their spare room again, but with Mum so poorly in hospital, I didn't want to be too far away from her. My brother was staying in Eastbourne too, so at least I'd have help if I needed it.

One week post-op

It was a relief to be feeling as well as I did. I was having to remind myself to rest because I felt so good. Having the flip-flow valve was far more comfortable than a catheter bag. I had no bladder irritation and my pee was clear. I had a little bit of soreness underneath my penis where the urethra had been fixed and where the opening had been closed. Apart from that, I had never felt better post-surgery. Feeling well was a blessing as I was having to visit Mum in hospital and attend flat viewings. Not the ideal time to be moving home, that's for sure. I found a flat, ideally situated just around the corner from Mum. That would be a great help once Mum returned to her flat as I'd be nearby to keep an eye on her. I planned to move in the following month. If the catheter removal went as planned, I would return to Devon and get packing.

Two weeks post-op

Although things had started out well, by the end of the second week I began to have bladder issues again. The all-too-familiar urge to pee returned with a vengeance. I started to feel concerned – there was no bleeding or cloudiness of the urine, but I knew the urgency to go wasn't right. I also felt completely washed out and hot to the touch.

I contacted St Peter's. Mr Stephens recommended that I try to continue with the catheter. If it came out too early, the new repair in the urethra might fail, having not had enough time to heal. This wasn't the advice I wanted to hear because really I just wanted the awful catheter out. My bladder really did not like catheters, and I thought perhaps if it came out, then the issue

may be resolved. However, I also wanted to do whatever gave me the best chance of a successful recovery. Mr Stephens suggested that I keep the catheter in, but get my urine dipped to check for infection if the problem didn't settle.

I decided to remove the flip-flow valve and fit a catheter bag instead, for two reasons. The main reason was so that I could free-drain into a bag and not have to get up for a pee every ten minutes. The other reason was so that I could more easily check the colour and smell of my pee. A strong smell and floating bits are all signs of an infection. I wanted to keep a close eye on it, so that if I noticed signs of an infection, I could nip it in the bud with antibiotics.

A friend recommended I try D-mannose powder. D-mannose is the stuff found in cranberry juice that helps to prevent and treat urinary tract infections. It is available in powder or tablet forms, at more concentrated levels than in juice. Although it is a sugar, it is not an irritant like glucose (which, like caffeine, it is sensible to avoid post-op if you have a catheter).

I wished I had known about D-mannose earlier as it was a miracle cure for my easily irritated bladder. Within a couple of days of taking the recommended treatment dose, I felt so much better. My temperature returned to normal and my pee was nice and clear. I decided to leave the catheter bag on for a bit longer, and I carried on taking D-mannose at the preventive dose.

Three weeks post-op

The D-mannose got me through to the three-week post-op mark, where I could finally have the catheter removed. I had been asked to return to St Peter's in London to have one of their nurses remove it. I think the reason was in case I had the same

issues as I'd had last time, with the urgency increasing after removal of the catheter.

When I arrived at the hospital, the nurse called me straight in. I was hugely anxious – partly because of the memory of the last removal, when I almost pissed myself in poor Ryan's car, and partly in case my urethra failed and I couldn't pee at all. The nurse gave me an injection of antibiotic before removing the catheter. This had never happened before, and it seemed like a very sensible idea. Once again, having the catheter removed was incredibly painful. My bladder categorically does not like catheters.

I returned to the waiting room, under instruction to pass urine comfortably and sufficiently twice before leaving. It was hard to not flash back to January and what happened on removal then. I kept drinking but I wasn't getting the urge to pee. I decided to just try anyway, so I made my way to the toilet.

Standing, with my jogging bottoms around my ankles, I pointed Finn Jr. at the toilet bowl. I tried my best to relax and let go, but nothing happened. I closed my eyes and prayed to the God of urination to please not let my urethra fail. Blood was now pulsing in my ears and the only water my body was letting go of was a cold bead of sweat running down my face. Then, whoosh – a sudden spray of pee arrived, which completely missed the toilet and hit the side of the wall. It stopped as abruptly as it started. I gave up, cleaned up the mess I'd made and returned to the waiting room to drink some more water.

Half an hour later, now bursting for a pee, I shuffled back to the toilet for attempt number two. Once again, I stood, penis in hand, staring down into the toilet bowl with steely determination. This time, a stream as straight as an arrow shot into the toilet. I was pleased about the noise as it covered up my sobs of relief.

It's so hard to explain to people who take peeing for granted, but, trust me, the joy of peeing in the correct way is indescribably wonderful. It had never felt right to me to sit to pee. I remember my dad once catching me straddling the toilet facing the wall. I was ashamed – not that he had caught me, but ashamed of my body not working in the way I instinctively felt it should. Growing up, I thought it was just the convenience thing – maybe I was jealous of boys who could pee anywhere. It was only now, peeing the right way, standing up, penis in hand, that I fully understood it. The wide-legged stance, the angle of my arm, my penis resting in my palm, the embodied sense of the entire act, gave me a feeling of body congruence and gender euphoria.

Satisfied now that I was peeing well and relieved in so many ways, I decided I was ready to head out to the station. I would then be boarding a coach home to Devon. I found my anxiety rising again. I had brought incontinence pants with me just in case I had a repeat of the previous time. Things certainly did not feel the same as last time. There was no bladder urgency and I felt fairly confident that I would be okay. Still, on missing my first underground connection to Victoria, I felt a warm flush of nerves about being delayed further from the next available toilet.

By the time I arrived in Victoria station, I needed the toilet – not in a desperate way but enough to make me hurry to find one. Annoyingly, I took the wrong exit out of the underground and ended up having to walk back towards the rail station. Thank goodness Victoria had now made the toilets free. I hurried down the steps and into a cubical. I was too nervous to try a urinal yet, and besides, I hadn't shaved my penis for three weeks and didn't want to get mistaken for a werewolf!

This time, peeing was even better than the last: instant, continuous and problem-free. It was at this point, however,

that I noticed that both of my hands were incredibly swollen. I don't know how I had missed this before. Obviously, I had been distracted by my penis. It was only my hands and fingers that were swollen (all my fingers were the size of sausages). I felt okay and wondered whether the antibiotic injection could have caused this. I was also carrying a heavy backpack, so perhaps it cutting into my shoulders, combined with everything medically going on, had caused the swelling? I didn't want to have to return to St Peter's, so I decided to find a café, sit it out for a while, and see if my hands returned to normal.

After an hour's break, having food and drink, luckily my hands returned to normal and I felt fine. However, the urgency to pee was getting more frequent. I even had to stop halfway through eating and rush to the loo. Every time I went to the toilet, there were significant amounts coming out, so it wasn't a false alarm. I reassured myself that this was normal after a catheter coming out; it was still nothing like last time. There would be a toilet on the coach, which was why I had decided to take that mode of transport, and if it was still like this when I arrived home, I could go to my doctor. I walked the short distance over the road from the café to the coach station, making sure to empty my bladder one more time and praying the onboard coach toilet was working.

Once I was on the bus, things settled down. I think the urge to pee, combined with my fear of being too far from the toilet, was increasing my anxiety. Now on a coach, sat opposite the toilet, I felt much less anxious. Also, as I was near the toilet, I kept making myself wait longer, to combat the anxiety and help retrain my bladder. Bladder tone can often be poor after having a catheter and it takes time for it to return to normal. By the time I arrived home in Dawlish five hours later, I was peeing at a much more normal frequency.

After a good night's sleep in my own bed at last, I felt much more like my usual self. The next day I ventured out into town and felt confident enough to use a urinal. I'm glad there was nobody else in that toilet. Seeing me peeing with a huge grin on my face would likely have been a little disturbing.

Five weeks post-op

From there on in, things were uneventful recovery-wise. Without a catheter, I was able to move properly. I could bend to put on my shoes without pain. I could sleep on my side. I was largely back to normal functioning. Surprisingly, the wound in my scrotum was not painful or bothersome in any way. It felt great to be closed again, and for everything to be dry and neat between my legs.

Despite feeling well, I knew I must still take it easy. However, I had a flat to pack and a life to relocate. I began to pack my things as slowly as I could. I also delayed the move itself for another week, so that on the moving day I would be five weeks post-op. Luckily, I had amazing friends and help on hand.

The move was a step too far recovery-wise. I had taken it as easy as I could, but after the move I had the old familiar urgency to pee return. I also had pain again at the end of my pee stream. I felt cross with myself and worried that I had messed things up by doing things too soon. I was still taking the D-mannose at the maintenance dose, so I immediately increased that to the treatment dose. After a couple of days, the urgency and the pain stopped. It looked like I had managed to nip an infection in the bud. Now it had to stay this way. I wanted this surgery done and dusted. I had to stay well and stay issue-free; only then would I be listed for stage three.

Two months post-op

Despite the joy at the rehook-up success. I found myself sliding into my familiar post-op low mood. This was unsurprising, considering the worry around Mum's health and the upheaval of moving my entire life back to Sussex. I had drifted away from Erin and from Owen and Frankie. The last thing I felt like doing was dating; and with everything else going on, I just did not have the mental space for it.

As well as my mental health taking a nosedive, my physical health was also in rapid decline. I was having random days of frequency of urination again, and the familiar stinging pain at the end of peeing – not as severe as I had before, but alarm bells were ringing. Also, my penis had begun to drip wee. I was never able to empty at the end of peeing, and moments later my pants would be damp. I tried changing my post-pee shaking technique. I did the milking manoeuvre, suggested by other trans guys, to drain the last drips. However, nothing stopped the dripping. It also occasionally happened when I needed a pee – I couldn't hold it without some drips escaping. In the end, I had to buy incontinence pads (just the light ones) to catch drips, because I was starting to get paranoid that I smelt of pee.

Once again, I began to feel sad and frustrated, that once upon a time I'd been peeing fine, without any post-op dripping, and now everything seemed to be going wrong again. I'd been tested for infection and all tests had come back clear, which was a relief. However, this latest development made no sense whatsoever, especially as the onset of symptoms was random. I noticed strange things, such as eating fewer carbs, made the urination issues disappear, and I could, with careful diet and regular D-mannose, ease the frequency of these symptoms for brief periods of time. It was all very odd.

Three months post-op

By the New Year of 2018, at three months post-op and still having issues, I'd had enough. I contacted St Peter's and was given an appointment to see Mr Stephens. When I described what had been happening, he was a little baffled, especially at the random nature of my symptoms. His conclusion was that I might have another issue with the urethra. Perhaps the repair had reverted to how it had been before, or it had either narrowed or widened. Any of these things can cause irritation and frequency. The other reason, which I didn't like the sound of at all, could be that my bladder was reacting badly to having a lengthened urethra. Mr Stephens said that some people's bladders just don't adjust. Despite my successful first hook-up, it might be that my bladder was now too stressed to handle the long urethra without getting irritated. Listening to Mr Stephens brainstorm possible reasons, I bit my lower lip and swallowed hard, not wanting to sob at his desk.

Unfortunately, the only way to know for sure would be to have a look inside my bladder and urethra. Mr Stephens then presented me with a dilemma. He could list me for simple cystoscopy surgery as soon as possible to have a look. He would do this himself, and if an issue was found, fix it there and then. Alternatively, I could wait for a stage three date, with a full team of surgeons. He would do a cystoscopy first and if he found no issue with my urethra, they would fit the erectile device. If I chose the first option – to just have the cystoscopy – and no issue was found, then the wait for stage three would be longer. I would have to recover from that procedure first, and then be relisted for stage three.

This was such an agonizing decision. My symptoms were not as severe as the first time, but they were causing me a lot of

anxiety and frustration. However, physically I could live with them, for a short period at least. I therefore decided to opt to wait for the stage three date. I decided I'd rather give it the benefit of the doubt. I would rather wait and put myself in the position of being able to have the erectile device than have a situation where that couldn't happen yet. I agreed to be listed for stage three surgery, with the provision that if they found a urethra issue, the attempt would once again be abandoned.

Five months post-op

As the weeks rolled on, my urination symptoms remained. I managed them as best I could with the D-mannose and oxybutynin. The oxybutynin was helping me to get some sleep, because when my symptoms flared up, I was needing the toilet every half hour or so.

I was a wreck by this point. I was so fatigued that I could barely lift my head off the pillow. If it hadn't been for the urge to pee, I likely would never have got out of bed. I had shelved all plans to return to my voluntary work. I had hoped, on returning to Eastbourne, to pick up some youth centre work. I loved my volunteer youth work in Exeter and only stopped because of having to travel back and forth to look after Mum. My mental health and my fatigue made any plans impossible. I had just enough energy to look after Mum's needs, and nothing left for myself. Mum's dementia had got rapidly worse, and we had to make the difficult decision to move her to a nursing home. My brother and I found her a lovely place, so at least she would be getting the care she needed. I had hoped that the knowledge of Mum being in good hands would help me to get my life going again. I needed to make new friends in Eastbourne and

build a new life for myself. However, I was just too poorly to do anything.

I began to think that there was more to the bladder issues and my health. Whilst I knew my mental health fluctuated, especially after surgery and particularly considering the circumstances with Mum, something felt off. I know myself very well. Years of practice of managing my mental health has given me a great deal of self-awareness. The way I was feeling was not like my usual mental ill-health or my post-op depression.

I tried to explain this to my new GP. Unfortunately, as he didn't know me, all he saw were my notes. He saw a trans person with a mental health history. He therefore concluded that all my issues were either down to my transition or to my mental health. Despite my protests, he just sent me away with new antidepressant medication. Eventually, after many visits resulting in just a higher dose of medication, I broke down in frustration. He finally agreed to investigate further and ordered blood tests. A week later, the results came back showing that I had hypothyroidism (an underactive thyroid). This, I was told, was why I had been so utterly exhausted.

After a few weeks taking levothyroxine, I started to feel much better. Most surprising, though, was that my urination issues began to clear up. I stopped needing to get up to pee during the night, and the pain at the end of urination disappeared. I emailed Mr Stephens to tell him about my new diagnosis. He said that the thyroid issues could have been the cause all along for my urine frequency. The thyroid is a tiny little thing with a powerful effect. Fatigue, heart flutters, anxiety, depression, numbness in the fingers, and urine frequency are just some of the symptoms of hypothyroidism. Perhaps I didn't have a urethra issue at all. For the first time in a while, I began to feel optimistic.

CHAPTER 12

The Gay Experiment

Although I wasn't happy about having a new health diagnosis, knowing why I had felt so awful was of some help. To know that I would soon feel better, once the new medication kicked in, was a great relief. This, combined with my optimism that the urinary issues might also be thyroid-related, helped to lift my mood. After months of feeling awful, I could finally see some blue sky behind the clouds. I was determined that now was the time to pick my life back up and I wanted to carry on with my dating adventures.

Ordinarily, I might have waited until I was fully well and my urinary issues completely resolved. However, I had learnt by now that life was too short to wait. And besides, Erin had shown me that being 'unfinished' did not have to be an issue with a person who was respectful and understanding. I did still have a lot on my plate, waiting for my health to improve and looking after Mum. Although she had settled into her new nursing home now, there was still a lot to do in terms of supporting her, taking care of her finances and so on. But I couldn't let this stop me. Instead, I would just be honest and upfront with whomever I might date.

Didn't that make for more honest interaction? So often, when dating, we are so desperate to present our best selves that we sacrifice our true selves. I would just be me from the start – a fatigued emotional wreck with a slightly drippy willy – and if they didn't like it, their loss.

I still wasn't looking for a relationship. I felt I had far too much to work out to settle down just yet. I still couldn't be sure that I was attracted to men. It wasn't so much that I needed a sexuality label, but that I needed to understand my sexuality story. For years I had been convinced that the reason my relationships with men had failed pre-transition was that I wasn't sexually attracted to them. I had come out as a lesbian many years prior to transition, because of my repeated failed attempts to get close to men sexually. I'd been so confused. I fancied men, or so it seemed, until we had sex, and then it all started to go wrong. Sex with men felt so wrong in ways I couldn't properly explain at the time. How could I feel an attraction, but then feel so repulsed once I tried to be intimate?

I had concluded that my inability to be intimate with men must mean that I was attracted to women. I began to experiment, dating a few women here and there, but I always ended up returning to men. Although being intimate with women felt more comfortable than with men, something still hadn't felt right. However, in 2006, I'd decided enough was enough. I exploded out of the closet as a proud butch lesbian and I swore off men forever. It wasn't until I realized that I was transgender, in 2010, that my sexuality made sense. The reason why being a lesbian hadn't felt quite right was that I wasn't a lesbian. I was a straight man. Or so I had thought.

Jen had thrown a spanner in my understanding of myself when she began living as Alex. Because I was still able to love Jen as Alex, I had to accept that I might not be as straight as I

had assumed. And, of course, my experiences with Owen and Frankie had confirmed that I wasn't straight. But I also didn't know if I was gay – at least, not completely. It didn't matter in terms of the label but it mattered in terms of making sense of my past.

We all tell ourselves stories to make sense of our past. It's human nature to do this, so that we have a sense of where we've been and who we are. I'd made sense of my past failings with men by understanding that I'd confused admiration for desire. My then unconscious knowing of myself as male manifested in a fascination with men. I didn't fancy them; I wanted to be them. But, considering my new experiences, was this story I'd told myself still true?

There was no denying that sex with Owen and Frankie had been wonderful, but what if the attraction worked with them because they were transgender? I do not mean in any sense that being trans is less than being a man. Owen identified as a man, and I very much saw and experienced him as a man. What I mean is that, as trans people, we have a common understanding, a shared history. Perhaps the common understanding was part of the attraction. I wondered whether I would have the same experience with a man without a trans history. Or, would I have the same experience as I'd had before I came out as a lesbian? It was this that I needed to find out, once and for all, so that I could then better understand my past and my new way of being attracted.

With these questions in mind, I focused on finding a cis gender man to date. No more playmates for now – I wasn't in a fit state for that anyway. I needed to rule out if there was a genuine attraction to men, or if Owen had been an exception. I bit the bullet and created myself a Tinder profile – classy, I know. After much deliberation, I decided that I wouldn't put that I was

trans on my profile. I figured that might either scare people off or attract fetish chasers. I would rather meet someone and then let my being trans come up naturally in conversation as we dated.

One afternoon, I received a notification that I had been 'matched' with a chap called Jamie. I scanned his profile. He was a year older than me and lived nearby in Brighton. The selection of pictures on his profile thankfully lacked the half-naked, heavily filtered selfies which were a feature of far too many of the other profiles. Jamie looked like a regular, genuine, down-to-earth guy. He had warm brown eyes and a kind but cheeky smile. He was handsome too. We began to message back and forth. He made me laugh and we chatted easily.

After a few days chatting, Jamie asked me when I had come out. This was my opener. I had thought I would tell a date in person about me being trans. However, it was more important to me that it just came up naturally, and this was the perfect opening. I paused, took a deep breath, and began to type: 'Well, that is one incredibly complicated question to answer. I came out first in my twenties...as a lesbian...'

Silence.

Then three dots began to blink on and off, indicating that Jamie was typing. It seemed like an age before a message finally appeared on my screen: 'Not many people stump me for words. You've had a rough ride, I'm guessing?'

His response told me all I needed to know. There were no inappropriate questions about what was in my pants, just a genuine understanding of what the emotional aspect of trans-ition must be like. I was so relieved. I had been afraid that a gay man might not want anything to do with me as a trans guy. And I feared that with someone who knew little about trans lives, I might be faced with awkward questions and thoughtless remarks. Jamie was the perfect gentleman and reassured me that

I need not be worried. He signed off with 'We won't be stuck for stuff to talk about over coffee, will we?!'

A week later, we arranged to meet for coffee in Brighton. My insides were like a sack full of excited kittens. Jamie was all smiles at the station as I bounced over. We headed to a café and chatted as easily in person as we had online. There were no awkward silences. The only awkward moments were me getting my head stuck in my pullover. I am not the king of dates. There were no questions at all about my being trans; it was as if it didn't even matter to Jamie. He didn't ask me any transition questions at all, until we interacted with the barista.

'What can I get you gents?' he asked.

Ordering for us both, Jamie replied, 'A flat white and a latte, the latte with soy milk please.'

We wandered into the courtyard of the café to find a table. Once we'd sat down, Jamie looked at me intently. 'How does that feel for you, being called "gent"?' he asked. 'I guess it must feel amazing.'

My heart lit up. Once again, Jamie's only concern was about my experience of being trans. It felt amazing to be seen and accepted as me, not as some novel fascination. He had me at this moment.

Eight hours later, after what we'd intended to be a two-hour date, Jamie saw me off at the station. We stood on the platform, staring at each other. I had no idea what to do. Should I kiss him? Was it okay for two men to kiss in public? This was Brighton, but still, having never kissed a man, as a man, in a public venue before, I had no idea what to do. And what if the kiss wasn't welcome? I panicked, and before I could decide what to do, Jamie kissed me on the cheek. I flushed with excitement, said goodbye, then promptly got on the wrong train home. Dammit!

On our second date, having already voiced my regret to

Jamie about not kissing him, I was nervous. We went for a drive through the countryside and up onto Devil's Dyke, which, yes, is a real place just outside Brighton. I was glad to be somewhere private. We sat on the grass, silently watching the last light of the sun bleed across the horizon. Lost in the moment, I was taken aback when suddenly, Jamie pushed me onto my back and kissed me. Not that I minded one bit, of course.

The kiss confirmed without a doubt that I was attracted to Jamie. But I had been here before in the past. I could be attracted to men, and I could even kiss them and feel aroused, but when it came to the sex, things fell apart. All men before my recent experience with Owen, regardless of initial attraction, had failed. What if this was a repeat of that past? It didn't feel the same, though. I was deeply attracted to Jamie. As we spent more and more time together, that attraction grew even more. My whole body was on fire every time he was anywhere near me. When we kissed, it was as much as I could do not to tear his clothes off. But Jamie wanted to take things slowly. I respected that. I was impatient, but I respected it. However, it did mean that I still had a question mark over the validity of my attraction. I wouldn't know for sure until we took the relationship to the next level of intimacy.

Finally, on a weekend at mine, it happened. I have never been so nervous about being naked. Jamie and I were lying on my bed cuddling, which mainly involved my not-so-subtle attempts to dry hump Jamie's leg. I hopped up to go to the bathroom, and when I returned, Jamie was in bed, and his clothes were on the floor.

'Are you naked?' I asked.

Jamie looked at me and grinned. 'Shall I get naked?'

More grinning.

My mind erupted into a tornado of thoughts. What if, once

naked together and he touched me, the attraction disappeared like it used to? What would Jamie think of my body? Here was a cis man, with a penis he had been born with. What if my body and my penis didn't match up? I couldn't get erect yet. Would that turn him off? But the experiences with Erin came to mind. I was enough. My body was enough. And, if I wanted to find out if the attraction would stay, then I just had to be brave and try, didn't I?

'Sod it!' I yelled, laughing. I ripped my clothes off with lightning-fast speed and jumped into the bed before Jamie could have a chance to see me naked. I had a cheeky peek under the covers at his penis. This was the first penis I had seen –for pleasure purposes at least – since 2006.

'Oi, cheeky!' said Jamie.

I wrapped myself around Jamie and kissed him deeply. The warmth of his skin against mine was electric. I reached for his penis and then our bodies became a swirling mass of heat and movement and Jamie was inside me. All the fear melted. To feel Jamie's strong arms around me, and his rough beard against my face, felt completely right. A missing piece of the jigsaw clicked into place. I knew exactly who I was and who I was attracted to. It was men, it had always been men, I was gay.

That's not to say that I hadn't enjoyed my time with women. I had enjoyed my time with Erin and I clearly had the ability to be attracted to all gender identities. However, in comparison, everything about the male body attracted me in a more complete way than being with a woman ever had. In that first sexually intimate connection with Jamie, my entire sexual history made sense. Of course, my sexual relationships with men had failed in the past because they had been relating to me as a woman. It was no surprise, therefore, that I had felt repulsed. Now, in being my true male self, I was being related to correctly in sexual

encounters with men. The attraction to women had allowed me to play the male role, and to therefore feel more male, which is why sex had been better with women than with men pre-transition. Just as I had come to realize that I had been a man all my life, now I came to realize that I had been a gay man all my life. I just had to go through transition to realize that.

My gay experiment didn't just surprise me with the realization that I was gay, but also with falling in love. I hadn't been looking for a relationship but I found one. I felt like I'd known Jamie all my life. Before long, we were spending alternate weekends at each other's flats. By the end of the month, we had said that four letter word to each other. Falling in love with Jamie was as easy and comfortable as climbing into a hot bubble bath. Not only had I discovered I was definitely attracted to men, but I had found the man I wanted to spend the rest of my life with.

It's funny how everything in my sexual summer had prepared me and led me to this moment. I would never have felt confident enough in my body had it not been for Erin. Thanks to my experiences with her, and with Owen and Frankie, I had been able to relax enough to take the huge risk of stepping into those uncharted waters with Jamie. Erin had helped me to overcome years of sexual shame. Now Jamie helped me to overcome years of sexual confusion. I could now even be grateful to Alex. Despite the way we ended, I was thankful to Alex, who had sparked off a chain of events which would ultimately lead to me finding an even larger truth about myself. Life really does have a peculiar way of unfolding in exactly the right way.

My relationship with Jamie, like with Erin, further helped in lessening my gender dysphoria. Jamie particularly helped me to develop an even greater confidence in my masculinity. It wasn't in anything he said, but in his relation to me that I

found my sense of self strengthening. Jamie had been gay his entire life and had only had relationships with men. This was a huge confidence builder. It confirmed that of course there was nothing female about me. I knew this, but dysphoria is a tricky beast whose effects can outwit the most powerful logic. Jamie also hadn't had any experience with trans people, meaning he wasn't practised at seeing people with different bodies. Therefore, I knew that he was seeing me for what was right there in front of him: a man. Every time Jamie looked at me, kissed me, or touched me, my maleness was asserted and with that there was an ever-decreasing level of dysphoria.

This new sense of self-assured masculinity made other things make sense too. It helped me to better understand the confusion I had felt when Alex came out and began living as male. At the time, I thought it was resistance to being back in a vulnerable position in terms of having to be openly gay. Whilst there had been some worry about that, I could see now that the bigger factor was internalized homophobia. I had been desperate to be seen as a 'real man' and I felt that as a gay man I wouldn't be viewed that way. It is quite common for gay men to be feminized and that was the last thing I wanted. I wanted to be a regular guy, and a regular guy was a straight man. It pains me to admit that these were once my feelings.

I had also been very resistant in terms of how my personality had been developing. I had been becoming increasingly more flamboyant. I was often mistaken for being gay long before I knew I was. I resisted this because I was afraid of being seen as less than a man. As trans people, our masculinity is often called into question and our traits and mannerisms are more heavily scrutinized. I especially felt this in terms of being both trans and gay. Although I don't see this as much as I once did, there have been a lot of unhelpful reactions towards gay trans men from

other trans men – that somehow, in being gay, we aren't 'trans enough' and therefore not 'male enough'.

The issue of visibility, then, was less to do with safety and more to do with how I would be perceived. My being with Alex and therefore gay, combined with my softening personality, once again put me at risk of being seen incorrectly. I risked being seen as a feminized man, and that to me was less than a 'real man'. It was for these reasons that I had been most resistant to being labelled a gay man.

I could see how for years, subconsciously, I had squashed any hint of feminine traits because of my desire not to be seen as female or related to as female. Being a lesbian had allowed me to play a butch role and to assert my masculinity, which had otherwise been invisible pre-transition. However, with my growing body confidence and sense of assuredness in my masculinity, I no longer felt the need to have to be a certain way to be seen as the man I am. I absolutely knew now that I was a man, however I acted and whomever I dated. I was finally able to embrace all of me, the me I hadn't realized I had been hiding. First Erin had unlocked the sexual me, and now Jamie unlocked the authentic me. The arm-waving, unicorn-riding, pink-t-shirt-wearing, unapologetically-in-touch-with-his-female-side gay man.

Settling into our lives together felt wonderful. Jamie was not in the least bothered about the fact that my surgery was yet to be finished. And he was equally accepting about all the health concerns which were still going on. By this point, the levothyroxine had helped a great deal. My fatigue was much more manageable and my mental health had improved. My better mood was also likely helped by all the love and lust that was going on. I was still having a bit of a dripping issue after peeing, but nothing as severe as it had been.

Once again, when nicely settled back into my life, the call for

surgery came. The familiar mixed feelings arrived: the need for this surgery to be done but also the worry. What if it went wrong again? And what about me and Jamie? We were in such a good place and surgery would have a huge impact on our relatively new relationship.

We Have Lift-Off

Stage Three Success

Before surgery could go ahead, I needed my thyroid levels to be in the normal range. If the thyroid isn't working properly, it can cause complications with healing. Therefore, my date for surgery was entirely dependent on having a satisfactory blood test. Luckily, my bloods came back as okay. My GP – a new one, who was particularly good at listening to me – wrote a supporting note to say she was happy that I would be able to manage the surgery. One hurdle over at least.

I was terrified of a repeat of the previous stage three attempt. Although my urinary issues seemed much better, the fear was still there. I was at least more hopeful, with Mr Stephens saying that my hypothyroidism may well have caused my urinary issues. Up until my underactive thyroid diagnosis, I had been convinced I would need another urethral fix, but perhaps I wouldn't need one after all. Still, I didn't dare to be excited. This time, the lead-up to the surgery day was very different; I had to manage my expectations, just in case.

Jamie was being incredibly supportive. He knew what had happened the previous time and how badly it had affected me.

The last thing I wanted was a failed attempt and for me to spiral back into depression. I worried about putting too much on Jamie's shoulders when we had only been together a short while. He told me not to be daft, that he loved me and wanted to be there for me, however things turned out. It was a relief and a reassurance to know that, this time, I would have someone with me, in any eventuality.

One of the most wonderful things about all this was that I didn't have to worry about how my partner might respond to my having an erection. What I mean is, with Alex, I had the concern that he might not like my adapted body and my new penis. As he had only been attracted to women before I transitioned, we didn't know how my having a penis would affect him. Jamie, however, was a gay man, who, by definition, was an enthusiastic fan of penises. Therefore, I had no worry at all about how this surgery would affect us. If anything, it would be a very welcome change.

At a meeting with Mr Stephens after my rehook-up a few months back, we had discussed the erectile devices. I hadn't had an opportunity to discuss this previously – I had just assumed the team knew best which device to fit. However, it seemed that as there were a couple of devices that would suit the shape and size of my penis, I could choose. My options here in the UK were between AMS and Coloplast pumps. I didn't know an awful lot about the devices, and quite honestly, I trusted the surgeons to know best. Mr Stephens had said there wasn't a huge amount of difference between the two. Both were three-part devices containing a reservoir, which would be in my lower abdomen, the pump, which would be housed in one testicle, and the cylinder, which would be placed inside my penis. Most trans guys who have RFF phalloplasty only have one cylinder. There is rarely enough room for two. The way the devices work is that

the reservoir holds saline solution, which you pump into the cylinder by squeezing the bulb housed in the testicle. You then press a button on the side of the bulb, to release the fluid back into the reservoir.

The main differences between the AMS and the Coloplast devices were in the materials and the pump. The Coloplast pump was rounder and the button smaller. The AMS had a squarer design and the button was much bigger and easier to find to deflate. The cylinder of the AMS was a much softer and more pliable material than that of the Coloplast. Mr Stephens told me that the AMS results in a much softer penis in the flaccid state and might be marginally less rigid than the Coloplast in the hard state.

Deciding between the two was tricky. Ultimately, I wanted to leave the surgeon who performed my surgery to decide. However, I was more drawn to the AMS because I preferred the material. The Coloplast's material was rather like that of a plastic straw and the AMS's material was rather like that of a balloon. It seemed logical, then, that the AMS device would mould better when soft, given the more pliable material.

I preferred the idea of a softer flaccid penis because I had some concerns about how my penis might be changed with the erectile device fitted. As trans men, we are showers not growers. What this means is that we are always the same size, whether flaccid or erect. A pump just makes us hard; it doesn't make us grow in length. I had already had to get used to packing 5½ inches into my pants. What if it became more difficult once the erectile device was fitted? I thought perhaps the AMS might allow my penis to feel more comfortable in my pants.

I loved the way my penis looked and hung, and I wanted it to stay as natural looking and feeling as possible. The Coloplast device may have made my penis more rigid and not hang and

swing as nicely as Finn Jr. currently did. I said to Mr Stephens that of the two, I preferred the AMS but that I would leave the final decision to the surgeon on the day, who would be able to better see which device may fit me best.

This time, the surgery would be performed by a new surgeon on the team, Mr Jansen. I hadn't met him, but I'd heard good things. I would have a camera inserted into the urethra first, just to make sure there weren't any problems. If the urethra was issue-free, then I would have the erectile device fitted.

Jamie and I headed to London the night before the surgery on Tuesday the 7th August, 2018. We would be staying at an Airbnb. I had an early arrival slot and I wanted to be as calm as possible. Plus, Jamie would be staying in London and helping me get back home. We needed somewhere for him to stay for the one night I would spend at the St John & St Elizabeth Hospital.

On the morning of the surgery, I was incredibly grateful to have Jamie by my side as the nurses ran through the usual pre-op stuff. I did my best to stay calm and to be open to any outcome. If they found an issue, I reminded myself, it wouldn't be a step back, it would just be a fix, meaning that I was still moving forward. I had to keep myself focused and prepare myself, just in case. Jamie hugged me, told me he loved me and reminded me that we were a team, and we would deal with whatever happened.

Later, on coming round from the anaesthetic, I cannot clearly remember how I discovered that the surgery had been successful. All I remember is being wheeled back to my hospital room and seeing Jamie sat in a chair, waiting expectantly. The nurses asked me to slide myself back onto the bed. I grinned at Jamie and said, 'I've got an erection!'

I lifted the loose white sheet and stared at the very obvious mound between my legs. Finn Jr. was standing to attention very

proudly. I was overcome with an overwhelming sense of relief and utter joy.

Day 1 post-op

The following morning, Mr Stephens visited, which confused me a bit. He was taking over from Mr Jansen, so I would be under his care for my discharge. Mr Stephens had a look at my penis to make sure everything was okay. He wanted to make sure that I was inflated enough, but not so much that my urethra was restricted. The device would be left inflated for ten days, so it was important I could still pee with it. He gave the go-ahead to remove the catheter and drain, and as long as I could pee without issue, I could go home.

Peeing with a boner is no easy task. I had to kind of lean into the toilet, so that I could get the stream into the toilet bowl rather than on the wall and floor. My pee was slow to come out, but the nurse reassured me that was normal and would be okay. I could go home.

Whilst peeing, I heard Jamie arrive. I was dressed by this point, in the loosest jogging bottoms I could find, but they didn't do the best job at hiding my boner. I opened the bathroom door. Jamie looked at my trousers and then burst out laughing. 'Wow babe, are you pleased to see me?' he said.

To see his reaction made my entire body light up with joy. This was wonderful, I had an erection and a partner who loved that I did.

Now we had the fun task of making it home on public transport without being arrested for public indecency. I thought I had bought baggy joggers, but it seemed they were not loose enough as they were not hiding my hap-penis. Luckily, I had brought a

light scarf with me. I draped the scarf around my neck, hanging down in front of my crotch. The bus stop was a brief walk from the hospital. It was an easy bus journey to the station, and then one train home. Although it would have been easy, had I not had to try to hide my bulge, Jamie had brought an umbrella with him, so he used that to shield people out of my way and hide me from view. I think we likely stood out more this way, with me shuffling down the street and Jamie wielding a giant rainbow umbrella like a shield. My knight in shining gay armour.

Making it to the station, I was desperate for the toilet. I tried to go, but it felt like I couldn't empty my bladder. I told myself that it was likely nerves. I was in a public place, with a boner, so it was no wonder my bladder was pee shy, even in a cubical. However, the issue kept getting worse all the way home. I spent most of the journey on the toilet, squeezing as much pee out as I could. By the time we were finally at home, barely a drip was coming out. I was beginning to go into a cold sweat and panic. What had happened was that the swelling in my penis had been aggravated by our journey home. Now the swelling, combined with the boner, was restricting my urethra. If I didn't sort it out fast, I would be in serious trouble.

I contacted St Peter's to ask what to do. At first, they suggested that I make my way back to London. There was no way I could manage that. By now I was bursting for a pee. I was going to cause myself damage if I left it the two hours it would take us to get back. Mr Stephens was in touch a few minutes later. He suggested that I try to deflate my device, just a tiny bit, to see if that relieved the pressure on my urethra. He sent me a link to a YouTube video, showing how to find the button on the device and deflate it.

Jamie was as cool as a cucumber through all this and he began to watch the YouTube video so he could help. In the

meantime, I cut the top off a large plastic water bottle and got into the bath so that I could catch the pee when I deflated.

'I think you're going to have to hold the bottle whilst I deflate,' I said to Jamie.

So, Jamie held the bottle under my penis, ready to catch any drips. Then, I began to feel around my testicle with the pump in, to try to find the button. Luckily, I wasn't too swollen, otherwise this would likely have been more painful and difficult to do.

'I think I've got it...'

And I had. I pressed the button and felt the instant relief from my nagging, full-to-bust bladder...and then started peeing with the velocity of a fireman's hose. There was no holding it, nor directing it. I missed much of the bottle, instead peeing over Jamie, and I couldn't stop. Well, there was no doubt about our closeness after this experience.

One week post-op

The following days were much less eventful. There was little pain and very little to heal from. I had three incisions: the biggest on my right side where they inserted the reservoir, and an incision either side of my groin where they inserted the erectile prosthesis and pump. They'd gone along the same incision line that they'd created at stage one, so at least I wouldn't have an additional scar. The only pain I had was in my right side where they had put the reservoir for the pump. It felt like a bad stitch, and it was painful to stand up straight. However, after a few days that settled down and, other than the odd twinge, the pain there disappeared.

My penis and scrotum didn't feel as sore as I thought they might. It helped that, because of the peeing incident, I was a little less erect than I would ordinarily be. The left ball with

the testicle implant was swelling and turning purple-blue. The implant was also rather high up, but I thought perhaps that was the swelling. This new testicle was sore but not at an unmanageable level. The right testicle with the pump in, surprisingly, considering I'd had to grope it and squeeze it to find the button, wasn't that swollen at all. Perhaps because it had already had an implant in before having the pump, it was less traumatized than the left one.

My main concern at this point was that I was dripping from my penis. It wasn't just dripping straight after a pee either, but also at random times. I hoped that this was because I couldn't shake and drain my penis in the usual way after peeing. Or, it might have been that, because of the swelling, urine was collecting somewhere. Though I wasn't overly concerned at this point, I was aware that any pee left collecting somewhere in my pee pipe could cause infection. So, I made sure to spend plenty of time with no pants on, just sat on a bed protector, so that any urine could drain straight out.

Other than having a bit of a waddle due to my swollen left testicle, I was able to move around easily and look after myself. Jamie stayed with me regardless, doing my washing, cooking for me, and being an absolute sweetheart. It was wonderful to share this with him. I thought that I'd be done with my surgery before I embarked on a serious relationship. However, to go through this final stage, to complete my journey with Jamie by my side, made it feel even more special. I was also extremely excited to soon be able to take Finn Jr. for his first test run.

Two weeks post-op

Just before reaching two weeks post-op, I was due to head to London to have my device deflated. As much as I was enjoying

my boner – it was supplying many laughs for Jamie and me – I was looking forward to not having to shield my hap-penis from the general public.

The usual procedure here in the UK is that the nurse first deflates the device, then shows you how to pump it up and release it. I had heard many guys say this was excruciating. The swelling and bruising often made the deflation difficult. Many people had to return later on, to be shown how to inflate, because it was too painful for them to try on the first attempt. I was optimistic that because of my lack of swelling, my experience might not be too bad. However, just in case, I decided to take some painkillers. I had some codeine left over from earlier surgery. I rarely use strong painkillers, especially once out of hospital. As a person in recovery from addiction, I must be careful what I take. I usually only use over-the-counter medications once I'm at home.

As it turned out, I needn't have worried at all. Whilst having the nurse handle and squeeze my testicle wasn't comfortable, neither was it painful. However, having to lie on the nurse's table – with my penis and testicle in hand – whilst she instructed me on how to inflate and deflate the device, was a tad awkward. I was also mortified that when the nurse squeezed my testicle, a bit of pee came out. You really do have to leave your dignity at the door with this surgery.

I could deflate the device easily enough, but I had a bit of trouble pumping it back up. The bulb kept slipping out between my fingers, which made me wince every time. The nurse reassured me that at first the bulb can be stiff, but that it would get softer and easier to pump over time as I got used to it. I would have to cycle the device, meaning inflate it and deflate it, three times a week, leaving myself inflated for 20 minutes each time. I couldn't have sex or masturbate for six weeks. This was going to be a long wait.

I asked the nurse about the issue I was having with dripping from my penis. She agreed that it was likely to do with swelling but that I should keep an eye on it. She also said that the device had likely changed the way I usually drain my penis after peeing. She advised that it might be that I just needed to get used to a new way to fully void after peeing. I also asked about the testicle on the left and she agreed it had been placed high up. If it didn't change after the swelling had gone down, she said, I could have a revision to lower it. She reassured me that I had healed incredibly well, but that I should still take it easy for the next few weeks.

Three weeks post-op

The nurse had told me to wait a few days after our appointment to begin cycling the device, just in case I was sore. However, after a couple of days, I felt fine and I was excited to play with it, so I decided to give it a try.

I sat up to do it this time (lying down had made grabbing my testicle and finding the button quite a challenge). I also made sure to sit on a bed mat so that if pee came out, I wouldn't soak everything. It was much easier to hold the testicle in place sitting up. I found the pump and tried to squeeze it. It was so stiff that it was hard to hold it and squeeze. The bulb kept slipping out of my fingers, which made me yelp every time. Finally, I successfully inflated the device and sat proudly staring at my erect penis. I hadn't been able to fully comprehend the impact of my erection until that moment. I realized I had been holding back from feeling the immense relief at completing my surgery. I had been terrified that something might go wrong, so I didn't dare celebrate too early. Even at three weeks post-op, I

still wasn't out of the woods yet. Infections post-implant surgery are common.

On having my penis fully erect for the first time, I was able to explore how he looked and how he felt. I noticed a couple of things which were of concern. One was that there was a large lump on my pubic bone. I assumed this was where the device had been anchored. The other issue was that when I stood up, not only did Finn Jr. point to the left, but he also pointed to the floor. He wasn't standing upright at all. To the touch, Finn Jr. was rock hard, so no problems there. He just wasn't pointing straight up as I had expected him to be. The angle all seemed to be with the way the device was anchored to my pubic bone. Anchored slightly to the side, it meant that rather than pointing up, Finn Jr. pointed left and slightly down. I also worried that the lump was a sign that the device wasn't anchored properly. Could that be making Finn Jr. less upright?

I messaged a couple of trans friends, and they said their penis was the same. They also had what they called 'the pump lump'. And, they also had a penis which hung lower. I was reminded that I was only a few weeks post-op and was swollen and heavier than usual, meaning the angle of my penis might be lower. I was also told that part of the reason for this is that we don't have the same muscles and tissues as cisgender males. This means we don't stand to attention in the same way. I felt relieved that it wasn't just me, but also a bit gutted. What if I had come all this way and it didn't work properly for sex? I still had three weeks before I could experiment, so I just had to put that worry out of my mind for the time being.

The swelling around my testicle had decreased significantly by this point. I could now definitely see that the new testicle was far too high. There seemed to be plenty of skin for it to move in, but it was stuck fast high up. The silicone implant also felt far

bigger than my original testicle. My first testicle was ping-pong size; the new one was golf-ball size. I had thought the swelling was making it seem bigger, but that seemed not to be the case. Testicle revisions are quite common, as they are not always the easiest things to get right and so much is dependent on swelling and body size. I was told it was an easy fix, so I decided to just give it a few months and see how it changed.

Now that the swelling had gone down, I was able to see how different Finn Jr. looked and felt with the device in place. When flaccid, with a cylinder inside, Finn Jr. felt quite different. There was far more substance to him now, he wasn't just floppy skin. Finn Jr. looked and felt far more like a penis, rather than just skin. Even Jamie commented on this when having a gentle feel one day. Mr Jansen had made the decision to use the AMS device and I was pleased he had. I couldn't feel the cylinder at all. I also loved that Finn Jr. still hung and swung naturally. Getting used to having more in my pants when I walked was interesting. By three weeks I hadn't yet made it back into jeans, but even in jogging bottoms I had far more of a bulge. I would have to learn to readjust all over again. I wasn't complaining, though.

Four weeks post-op

I continued to heal well in terms of the erectile device and the sutures, which was a relief. However, the mild itching I'd had in the early days post-op was now an insatiable burning itch which would not let up. I had initially thought this was caused by the hair growing back. Itching was common for me. I'm a hairy guy and so there is a lot to grow back after they shave me for surgery. I also get itchy around my stage one scars under my bum cheeks as they always swell up post-op. I just thought that the extreme

itching was a combination of the hair growing back and the swelling. And, I presumed that, like with my previous surgeries, the itching would soon stop. But it didn't; it only continued to get worse.

I made an emergency appointment with my local doctor. I wanted to make sure that I didn't have an infection. I was terrified, still, of erectile device failure due to infection. After a brief examination my doctor told me I had folliculitis. This means that the hair has been in-growing and become infected. The doctor prescribed some antibiotics and cream. I was hopeful that soon my balls would stop burning.

I had also begun to feel generally under the weather and exhausted. This could well have been due to the infection in my hair follicles and the fact that I wasn't sleeping properly because of the itching. But it was also common for me to have these low moods after surgery. It could also be my thyroid, having only recently got my levels back within the normal range. Perhaps surgery had sent those levels out of whack again. My doctor made me an appointment to have my blood tested in a couple of weeks, to assess whether I might need a higher dose of levothyroxine. At least these complications were just side effects and not anything to do with the erectile device itself, which was a relief.

Six weeks post-op

By six weeks post-op, my balls were no longer ablaze. The itching had gone completely, and the swelling had almost returned to normal. I could now fit back into jeans again, and I was loving the new, more visible line of my penis. I greatly enjoy the six weeks post-op feeling, where you suddenly turn a corner and begin to

feel more like your usual self. I had my blood tested at six weeks too, which confirmed my suspicions. My TSH levels had risen again, meaning my thyroid was struggling and I needed more levothyroxine. My doctor increased the dose, and I was hopeful of having more energy soon. At six weeks post-op, I could also breathe a sigh of relief at having managed to stay infection-free. I was now past the highest at-risk stage. The likelihood now of getting an infection was significantly reduced.

Having reached the magical six weeks post-op milestone, I was now able to play with myself again and to have sex. I was incredibly nervous, but of course very excited too. Having not had a wank in six weeks, I was getting desperate. Having a healthy sex drive can often be frustrating.

Wanking with a hard penis was an entirely unique experience. Just the way it looked to hold my erect penis in my hand was arousing enough on its own. The sense of my masculinity asserted, my body correctly shaped, all of this combined into a feeling of euphoria.

I discovered that there were now two ways I could wank. I could grip my penis and pull back and forth; or, using lots of lube, I could glide my hand up and down. Both ways felt amazing and both ways easily achieved orgasm. Without a foreskin, although my penis didn't move in the same way as a cis male's might, whichever way I wanked, my penis moved back and forwards over the cylinder placed inside. This new movement appeared to have increased the sensation. Now, I didn't even have to think about my base dick – I came without even having to incorporate it into the movement.

I could still access my base dick, although it was now a little more difficult as my giant, high bollock was in the way. But I didn't need to access my base dick. It was good to be able to feel the erection there when I was aroused, but other than that,

that part of me was now just part of my entire penis – nothing more or less than an area that felt good to the touch, but not one I relied upon.

Having become more confident in the way my penis now worked, I was keen to see how it fared during intercourse. This was one of the defining moments I had waited years for. However, this had now changed significantly from when I first started fantasizing about it. I had expected to be having sex with a woman, and here I was, a gay man with a boyfriend. My love of anal had led me to realize that I did love to be a bottom, but of course I wanted to try to top.

I was nervous because I had never done this before. Jamie had mostly been a bottom before we met, so he knew what he liked. What if I was awful at it? Jamie was understanding and supportive of my nervousness, reassuring me that everyone feels nervous when they lose their virginity. I hadn't taken the fact on board that this would be me losing my virginity as a man – my first time penetrating someone else with my own flesh.

Although I was 44 by this time, I was really an 18-year-old boy having his first sexual experience. Remembering this helped me to lessen the pressure a bit. I had to start with the condom, and having never put a condom on a penis before, let alone my own, that proved trickier than expected, especially with shaking hands. Doggy-style was going to be the easiest position for my first time, so I knelt behind Jamie and got into position.

I tried everything to get myself inside him. We tried lots of lube and various positions, but my penis wouldn't go in. It kept bending at the base and coming out again. Or, when I did get it in, I couldn't thrust properly, because yet again it would bend. And, I was having pain in the right side of my pubic bone where the pump was anchored.

My mind started to spiral into black thoughts. What if the

bend to the left meant that the pump was broken? What if after all this I couldn't have sex? What if it never worked? Before long, I had plummeted into the darkest tar pit of gender dysphoria, deeper than I'd been for years. In that moment, I became utterly convinced that that all this had been a waste of time. I would never be a real man; at best I was a woman with a penis.

It was such a shock to go at once to such a dark place. It was a shock to Jamie too, who had never seen me have an attack of dysphoria. For a few minutes I couldn't say anything and I shut down completely. Jamie held me and reassured me until I could eventually confess all of these feelings to him. It was so hard to share these thoughts out loud. What if I said them and he agreed or saw me differently?

'Munchkin, I love you, You are my man, with a very new penis. It's okay.'

We put off trying for a while after that. We returned to me bottoming because that was far less stressful for the time being. I needed time to make sense of what had happened, and to feel better able to deal with it

Looking back at this now, I put far too much pressure on myself. I had built up the expectation, imagining my first time to be special, fireworks going off, moving in time together, all these romantic notions. In truth, most first times are awkward, embarrassing and little more than a laughable first attempt. I needed to give myself time to play, to get it wrong, to learn to feel my way with a penis that I'd only had for a few years and only recently got erect.

Finally, on our second attempt, I got in with far less effort. Though there was still a ton of nerves. I was worried about hurting my new equipment and about hurting Jamie. I had never been inside anyone before, not with my own flesh. And the sensation wasn't enough to tell me exactly where my penis

was. Although sensation was still increasing and I had no issue with orgasm, the lack of direct tactile sensation meant I was thrusting blind. This would take time to get used to. It dawned on me that special didn't mean perfection. Special meant having a partner with whom I could share these first clunky attempts as we discovered new ways to be intimate together. Nothing could be more special than that.

Final Healing and Reflections on My Journey

The final healing from the last stage of phalloplasty took a fair few months. There wasn't just the healing; I also had to adapt to a new way of using my body. In the months that followed, I became more confident in my penis and his new abilities. Gradually, my initial concerns about the erectile device disappeared. Despite having surgery so many times, I could still forget how long it takes for a body to heal, and for me to adjust. We need a good chunk of time to heal correctly, yet it is all too easy to worry about things in those first few months.

A large part in finding confidence in Finn Jr.'s abilities was in getting to know and trust the erectile device. Although I had initially been worried about the angle of my penis, I later realized that by giving the pump a few extra squeezes, I could in fact make Finn Jr. stand far more upright. I had been too worried about over-pumping in the early days in case I broke the device. I soon realized that it was impossible to over-pump. My technique in pumping had also improved. I now knew that if I waited a moment or two after Finn Jr. was inflated, I could give him another pump to get an even firmer erection. I also

discovered that by pulling him upright when pumping, he would then remain much more upright. He still pointed outwards rather than up at the ceiling, but that's common for men.

The bend to the left remained when erect, but I had got used to that too. The angle is because the device is anchored slightly across my pubic bone, meaning that it is impossible for the device to stay pointing forward. Perhaps this is the only way it can be positioned. When Finn Jr. is flaccid, he points downwards and without a leftward bend. But as soon as the pump lets in saline solution, the firmness then forces the cylinder to the left. It does not affect the function, and so I have decided that it just adds character.

The leftward bend did mean that navigating my erection took a while to get used to. Thrusting straight forward to penetrate could cause a bend in the base of the device. Sometimes when this happened, it caused a bit of pain and a popping sensation (which initially made me panic). However, after a few months of experimenting, I learnt how to work with the way the pump moved. I did continue to get a bit of discomfort during and after penetration. Most of this pain was in the lump on my pubic bone where the device has been anchored. The lump has got smaller over time and the pain is now rare. The discomfort was where the pump device was settling in and embedding in my pubic bone. It seems to be much more solid there now, and it only causes me discomfort when I'm a little over-enthusiastic. The popping is just where the device bends, and it no longer freaks me out.

I worried about my testicles initially too. The right testicle with the pump device inside felt very odd in the beginning. Even though I had seen the erectile device before surgery, I hadn't connected that because the box is square, my testicle would be an odd shape. I can feel the edges of the box, but you can't in fact

see them, so it isn't an issue. The only time the square edges have given me a problem is when sat on an exercise bike in the gym. However, any man is going to need to rearrange his testicles to sit comfortably on a bike saddle. The left testicle is still incredibly high up. I would like it to be lower, but not enough to put myself through even the most minor of surgeries. I have decided to wait until I need my device fixed, and then ask about having my left testicle lowered. The scrotum may not look as perfect as I'd like, but in all honesty, I don't mind that much.

Thankfully, my urinary issues have not resurfaced. The dripping I'd had post-op turned out to be more to do with having to learn a new shake technique after the implant. It seems that with the new mechanics inside my penis and groin, the shape of my urethral pipe had changed. I now needed to push a spot just below my penis to expel the last few drips. I have learnt to not push too hard on that bit, though, otherwise I can easily jet a stream of pee up in the air. Not so great when you are peeing in public.

Looking back on those post-op concerns now, they were all to do with needing more healing time and learning to use the erectile device. Like with every stage of surgery, the tendency is to worry. The worry we feel is understandable. With the amount of time and effort we invest, of course we want everything to be okay. But a body needs time to heal and adjust. I also had to learn to be patient with myself when it came to sex and intimacy. As trans men, we have an especially huge learning curve. Not only do we have to heal, we must also learn how our new body configurations work, and we have nothing to compare this with. I am assured, by gay and straight men alike, that my early fumblings and mishaps are a normal part of the coming-of-age process.

The fact that my erection is mechanical has never bothered

me or Jamie. I have asked him if my penis feels any different and he says that it doesn't. However, Jamie does draw the line at pumping my device. As a cisgender guy, even the thought of squeezing a testicle makes him wince. I have got so quick at using the pump, though, that I can do it one-handed – without looking – whilst we are engaged in foreplay. So, having to pump has never felt like an inconvenience. It can also help with arousal to pump beforehand. Usually, an erect penis will let a partner know that you are in the mood. As my arousal doesn't always show, if I am in the mood, I will pump up so that Jamie can 'discover' my erection. It's also just great fun to walk around the house with a hard-on.

I am now approaching two years post-op from having the final stage of my surgery. And it's been five years in total since I began my lower surgery journey. It took many months for the reality to set in – that my surgical journey was complete. There would be no more waiting for surgery dates, no more pain and healing, no more changing body parts. My body was no longer a medical site; it was finally my own. Three years had, in retrospect, gone by incredibly fast. I finally had the penis I had dreamt of.

I am astounded at what my body can handle and how well it has healed. All my scars have now faded – even the stubborn ones under my bum cheeks. My arm recovery has been particularly incredible. I was lucky to have an arm graft which took very well. This is one of the areas that St Peter's have made the most progress with over recent years. New advances in techniques and medical dressings mean the grafts have a much better outcome than they once did. My arm looks fantastic. The scar outline is visible, but the graft itself is of even colour and great skin quality. Hair never grew back on it, though, save a few tufts here and there.

I recently decided to go ahead and have my arm tattooed.

The decision wasn't made to hide the scar, because to be honest it didn't bother me. Jamie said that it bothered him at times, but only because it broke his heart at what I'd had to go through over the years. The reason for the tattoo, for me, was more as a tribute to my body and to mark the end of my transition. My mum passed away not long after I completed my surgery. I wanted the tattoo to be a memorial to her too. After all, it was my beautiful mum who gave me this incredibly resilient body of mine. I chose a phoenix, wrapping around my forearm. I even had some of my mum's ashes blended in with the ink – telling people this either thrills them or makes them cringe. I love it. It's a fitting tribute to Mum and to my gender transition process. The graft is now no longer visible unless you study the tattoo up close.

Those three years of lower surgery were some of the toughest years of my life. In some ways, the journey was harder than I had imagined. To be constantly cycling between surgery and recovery is exhausting. Some of the setbacks, especially when I was reopened underneath, were utterly devastating and took me to the very edge of breaking point.

In those darkest of times, what kept me going was the knowledge that it would all be worthwhile in the long run. I had taken time to thoroughly explore surgery and my needs and this meant I owned those decisions 100 per cent. This is why my advice to anyone exploring lower surgery options is always to take your time. It is okay to have doubts and concerns. Working through them brings you to a stronger sense of certainty. That certainty, owning your decisions, will later be your superpower. When times get tough, and your body is alive with pain, that certainty will get you through.

Looking back now at the early days, whilst I was working through my decisions, feels very surreal. Those worries I had about sacrificing parts – and my worry about whether new parts

would work adequately – feel like a distant dream. My body now feels as if it has always been configured this way. Sometimes I feel around underneath my penis, as if touching certain parts will bring a memory of what used to be there. It never does. I have never missed or noticed that my vagina has gone. It feels as if a wound was closed and healed rather than having had something taken away.

Sensation, of course, was my biggest concern. It was impossible to imagine how sensation might feel. I worried that my new penis might not have enough sensation or that I would still have to use my old parts to orgasm. Neither of those things has happened. The sensation I have is more wonderful than I could ever have dreamt it would be. My base dick now is just an area which throbs and swells when aroused. I no longer think of it as my T-dick or my base dick; it's just a part of my penis.

It dawned on me not long ago that I had been thinking about sensation in terms of it coming back. But, of course, my penis is an entirely new body part. Sensation didn't grow back but instead arrived for the first time. Feeling Finn Jr. come to life is something I will never adequately be able to put into words. The more comfortable I have become in my body, the more pleasure I have been able to get from it. This is what I truly could never have imagined at the beginning of my journey. It isn't just my new penis which is giving me sensation; it's now my entire body. Previously, my dysphoria meant that pleasure always came with a side order of discomfort. Therefore, I had shut off parts of my body without even realizing. Now, pleasure is no longer limited, because I can touch and feel every single inch of my body without any discomfort whatsoever. It is this which has opened an entirely new world, a kaleidoscope of sensations, that I could never have imagined in my wildest dreams.

It's also hard to believe I was once put off the idea of surgery

by tales of monster penises. Finn Jr. is a handsome boy, even with his scars. There is absolutely nothing of Frankenstein about him. Penises are not the prettiest body part anyway – at least, I don't think they are. Besides, they come in all manner of shapes and sizes. In a penis line-up, Finn Jr. might not look exactly like a cis penis, but he looks incredibly close. What is important is that he looks good in his own right and looks just like a penis should.

This brings me to the question of whether there are things I would change. In all honesty, no. Okay, my scrotum isn't perfect, my left testicle could do with being lower, and my penis bends to the left when erect, but these are my beautiful imperfections. In many ways, having a few quirky bits on my body makes me more like everyone else. Who doesn't sometimes look at their body and see something they might like to change? I am 46 years old now, and gravity has taken its toll, alongside far too many tubs of ice cream. I am also covered in scars from my various surgeries. The difference now is that I am able to accept myself completely. These imperfections are nothing more than ordinary human niggles. They are not fuelled by gender dysphoria. To at last look in the mirror and see nothing but the man that I am – and always have been – speaks volumes about the success of this remarkable surgery. I don't know if the surgeons can ever fully comprehend what a difference they make to our lives. There will never be enough words to express the gratitude I have for the penis they created for me and the new life this has given me.

I do feel that a large part of phalloplasty is about managing expectations and getting to a place that is 'good enough'. Otherwise, we could spend our lives changing little bits here and there and never being happy. No penis is perfect. As for phalloplasty, it's never going to be a cis penis, no matter how

many advancements the surgeons make. I believe that part of preparing for phalloplasty is acknowledging that fact, and then working out what 'good enough' means for you.

That doesn't mean you shouldn't strive for the best outcome. There are so many advancements now in lower surgery. Many surgeons are willing to try new things to improve outcomes. There is even the option of medical tattooing post-surgery. Medical tattooing can give a more realistic appearance in terms of penis and glans colour, and the appearance of veins. However, there must still be a level of managing expectations, and of drawing a line under when enough is enough. Imperfections, and our gracious acceptance of them, are what make a body unique and beautiful.

I have worked hard on accepting my body and loving it as it is. I had to accept that my new genitals would never look and function in the way they would have done had I been born with them. Thank goodness for the serenity prayer as it has taught me a great deal about acceptance. I have the wisdom to know that there are parts of my body I can change and parts I can't. I have changed the parts I could and accepted the parts I can't. For me, 'good enough' meant being able to have a penis I could pee with and have penetrative sex with a partner. As long as it looked good enough to stand next to other guys at a urinal, and to make me smile when I looked in the mirror, that was good enough for me. As it stands, my penis far exceeds these expectations.

Surprisingly, being with Jamie has helped enormously with my acceptance. One of my biggest fears in being intimate with a cis man was that I would find it too dysphoric. I worried that my body would not compare and I would feel inadequate. I have never felt inadequate with Jamie. There are, however, parts of Jamie that I sometimes wish I had. Jamie has a particularly wonderful nutsack. I love the prominent blue veins which snake

across it. I love the way that it hangs. I love how it changes all the time. Sometimes it's tight and high up, other times it's loose. I would be immensely proud to own a scrotum like that. However, I never look at Jamie's glorious nuts and feel dysphoric. It's more of a fleeting wish. The fact that I can feel nutsack envy and be okay with that shows me that I have reached a place of acceptance, and that gives me much peace.

The larger question of course is, was all the time, pain and frustration of surgery worthwhile? Worthwhile, in this instance, means being free of gender dysphoria. The entire point of my going through lower surgery was to change my body so that it stopped causing me distress. Lower surgery has been remarkably successful from that point of view. However, the changes I have experienced, resulting in a body I am now more comfortable in, have not happened in a vacuum. Not only the surgery but also my experiences with my changing body have helped to lower my dysphoria and increase my body comfort.

Surgery is a vital part of the process of healing, but it is not the whole picture. Trying to reconnect with ourselves and overcome our past, in a body that isn't our home, is almost impossible. I could never have begun to work through my sexual shame and emotional disconnect before lower surgery. I doubt I would even have wanted to, because there was no true enjoyment to be had with my body. Surgery changes our bodies to ones that we recognize as ours and feel at home in. Once we feel at home and secure in our bodies, then the healing work can begin. Therefore, surgery is only one part of the healing process of overcoming dysphoria.

Dysphoria causes all sorts of other coexisting issues, especially for older trans people like me. I have many years of poor mental health to undo, and surgery doesn't automatically make that go away. Hormones and surgery are not a magic elixir that

can instantly propel us into a future which is free of mental health challenges and body insecurities.

Like with body acceptance, I feel that to overcome dysphoria and its associated issues, we must engage actively with the process. I don't believe we can just passively let surgery do all the work. I don't mean that everyone must go and find themselves a Sexological Bodyworker or engage in polyamorous play (though I highly recommend it!). What I mean is that we must be willing to face our dysphoria head-on and move through it as our bodies change. We must be willing to do the inner healing work and actively learn new ways to reconnect with our bodies.

I didn't know this when I began my journey. I certainly did not set out to have a life-changing sexual adventure. I had expected to spend my surgery years in limbo, patiently waiting for them to end before I could even think of exploring with my new body. It was in my experience with Erin that I discovered the powerfully transformative effects of stepping into the dysphoria and associated fear. I absolutely know that the success of lower surgery for me is a result of engaging fully with the process of healing from the past and in getting to know my new body. Courage isn't going through surgery. Surgery is a necessity. Courage is bravely stepping forward into uncharted waters with that new body, and then engaging with our growth and healing. That is the magical place where we begin to not only overcome gender dysphoria but to truly heal our entire selves.

Although I say that those three years were the toughest, they were also some of the best years of my life. Much of the joy that came out of them was most unexpected. I feel like my penis led the way and took me on a journey of healing I would never have otherwise travelled. It was entirely because I actively engaged with my healing and my changing body that this journey has been so incredibly profound and enjoyable.

So, the answer to the question of whether all the pain and frustration were worthwhile is an extremely easy and resounding yes. Now, all the awful complications have melted away in my mind, replaced by the joy of living in a body that feels like home. I can fully occupy every bit of space inside my body and feel an ease and a deep sense of peace. I had no idea this amount of space and sense of peace inside one's body was even possible.

At the beginning of this journey, I saw it as a means to an end. I was waist-deep in dysphoria and all I wanted was a body that I felt at home in. At the end of my journey now, I can see this journey was less of a means to an end and more of a means to a new beginning. In a body that is right for me, I have been able to heal from the past in ways that were inaccessible to me before. I have been able to find parts of me that were deeply hidden through years of sexual shame and confusion. Having a penis has set me free to walk into a new future, knowing fully who I am. Now the next adventure can begin.

Phalloplasty Surgery Essentials

The following items are things which I have found helpful through my phalloplasty journey.

Infection prevention/home hygiene

- A few large bottles of antibacterial hand gel. The ones with a pump are the best as they are easier to use with one hand after stage one. Keep a bottle next to where you sit, another beside your bed and another one in the bathroom.
- Make sure to have separate towels (including hand towels) for your sole use.
- Avoid using flannels as these can carry bacteria. Instead, use dry wipes that you dispose of after each wash. These are great to dry hygienically around wound areas too.
- Incontinence mats. Use these to protect sheets when in bed or sitting in a chair. They also provide a hygienic area for changing dressings and/or catheters.
- Disinfectant wipes for the toilet seat.

Personal hygiene

- Wet wipes – fragrance-free and as natural as possible.
- Antibacterial soap.
- Dry wipes for washing and drying yourself (see above).

Catheter care outdoors

When you have a catheter for an extended period of time, it is important to maintain hygiene when outside of your home. I found it helpful to create a small travel pack of the following:

- Mini bottle of antibacterial hand gel.
- Small pack of tissues.
- Small pack of wet wipes.
- Small pack of antiseptic wipes.

First-aid kit

- Basic non-adhesive dressings of various sizes for any wound emergencies.
- Micropore tape.
- Zoff® (or equivalent) adhesive remover makes taking dressings off so much easier and less painful.

Skin and scar care

- Tamanu oil.
- Kelo-Cote® scar gel.

- E45 cream.
- Castor oil.

Supplements

- Dissolvable high-dose vitamin C and zinc.
- D-mannose powder. Take a preventative dose when using a catheter and before urethral hook-up and throughout recovery. Move onto the treatment dose at the first sign of irritation/infection. If you have any questions or concerns about taking supplements, always check with a doctor or nutritionist first.

Clothing

- Baggy sweat/jogging pants.
- Loose boxer trunks.
- Short-sleeved front-button shirts. After stage one, these will be easier to put on over the graft arm.
- Slip-on or Velcro® slippers and shoes (you won't be able to bend to put them on yourself).

Other useful items

- Extra-long charging lead for phone/e-reader/tablet.
- Book-rest for propping up the above when you only have one hand.
- Phone-holder clip. This clips onto a table so you can position your phone and use it one-handed.

- V-shaped pillow. This is great for when you have to sleep slightly upright.
- Body pillow. Designed for pregnancy, this is great to help support you when sleeping on your side.
- Adjustable bed-rest to prop you up more securely than pillows can.
- Long-handled grab stick or sock aid. This is great to help with putting on shoes and socks.

Additional Resources

I have documented my entire lower surgery journey in both video and written form. My documentation may further help you in your exploration and journey.

My YouTube channel, FinnTheInfinncible, has a vast collection of lower surgery resources and contains my video diary throughout the entire lower surgery process. There you will find playlists for every stage, from deciding on lower surgery, to preparing for lower surgery and then through each stage of phalloplasty.

www.youtube.com/user/FinnTheInfinncible

My accompanying blog contains many phalloplasty resources too, including preparing for hospital, what to pack in your hospital kit bag, and first-hand accounts of recovery, healing and sensation progress.

https://finlaygames.com

For anyone who may be interested in working with a sexological practitioner, the following links contain more information.

https://www.trustedbodywork.com

https://www.somaticsexeducation.com/register-of-practitioners